Do-it-yourself

Will Kit

Guidance Manual

Important Facts about this Lawpack Kit

This Lawpack Kit contains the information, instructions and forms necessary to make your own Will in England, Wales, Northern Ireland or Scotland. It is important that you read and follow the instructions in 'How to use this Kit' on page 5.

There is an infinite number of provisions a person may make in a Will. The Will Forms included in this Lawpack Kit cover the most common ones, but we do not cater for all circumstances.

The information this Kit contains has been carefully compiled from reliable sources, but its accuracy is not guaranteed, as laws and regulations may change or be subject to differing interpretations. This is particularly true for any figures given, which are stated liable to change in the next Budget. The law and all figures are stated as at 1st January 2011.

Neither this nor any other publication can take the place of a solicitor on important legal matters. This Lawpack Kit is sold with the understanding that the publisher, authors and retailer are not engaged in rendering legal services. If legal advice or other expert assistance is required, the services of a competent professional should be sought.

As with any legal matter, common sense should determine whether you need the assistance of a solicitor rather than relying solely on the information and forms in this Lawpack Kit.

We strongly urge you to consult a solicitor if:

- substantial amounts of money or property are involved;
- you do not understand the instructions or are uncertain how to complete and use a form correctly;
- what you want to do is not precisely covered by the forms provided;
- you and your spouse have different domiciles;
- you own or have an interest in property abroad or have written a Will abroad.

The contents of this Manual have been approved by Leolin Price QC and Richard Dew of Ten Old Square, Lincoln's Inn, under English law, by Tughans solicitors under the law of Northern Ireland, and by Neill, Clerk & Murray, solicitors, under Scottish law.

EXCLUSION OF LIABILITY AND DISCLAIMER

Whilst every effort has been made to ensure that this Lawpack Kit provides accurate and expert guidance, it is impossible to predict all the circumstances in which it may be used. Accordingly, neither the publisher, author, retailer, the barristers and solicitors who have approved the contents of this Kit, nor any other supplier shall be liable to any person or entity with respect to any loss or damage caused or alleged to be caused by the information contained in or omitted from this Lawpack Kit.

Lawpack gives you a limited guarantee. If for any reason you are not happy with your purchase, you may return it to us with your receipt within 30 days of the date of purchase for a full refund. In no event shall our liability exceed the purchase price of this Kit. Use of this Lawpack Kit constitutes acceptance of these terms.

This Lawpack Kit may not be reproduced in whole or in part in any form without written permission from the publisher, except that forms may be photocopied by the purchaser for his or her own use, but not for resale.

© 2011 Lawpack Publishing Limited
PRINTED IN ENGLAND

Contents

How to use this Kit	5
Domicile	6
Making your Will in England, Wales & Northern Ireland	7
Why a Will is important	7
What is intestacy?	7
Who should make a Will?	8
How long is a Will valid?	8
When is it necessary to prepare a new Will?	8
Preparing to make your Will	9
Executors and trustees	10
Guardians	10
Beneficiaries	11
Adults	11
Minor children	11
Charity	12
Gifts	12
Specific gifts and legacies	12
The residuary gift	13
A replacement residuary beneficiary	13
Replacement gifts after gifts to children	14
Disposal of property during your lifetime	15
Property that does not pass under your Will	15
Joint tenancies	15
Other property	16
Tax considerations in estate planning	16
Witnesses to your Will	17
Signing your Will	17
How to revise your Will	18
Safekeeping of your Will	18
Using the England, Wales & Northern Ireland Will Forms	18
Glossary	19
Completed examples and worksheets	20
Making your Will in Scotland	32
Why a Will is important	32
What is intestacy?	32
Who should make a Will?	32
How long is a Will valid?	33
When is it necessary to prepare a new Will?	33
Preparing to make your Will	34
Executors and trustees	35
Guardians	35

Beneficiaries	36
Adults	36
Underage children	36
Charity	37
Gifts	37
Specific gifts and legacies	37
The residuary gift	38
A replacement residuary beneficiary	39
Disposal of property during your lifetime	40
Property that does not pass under your Will	40
Tax considerations in estate planning	41
Witnesses to your Will	42
Signing your Will	42
How to revise your Will	42
Safekeeping of your Will	42
What happens when someone dies?	43
Using the Scotland Will Forms	43
Glossary	44
Completed examples and worksheets	46

Template documents

Form of Letter to Executor	58
Funeral Wishes	59
Location of Important Documents and Summary of Personal Information	60
Important People to Notify	61
Property Inventory	62

Loose-leaf forms

For England & Wales and Northern Ireland:

Will Form 1 - Simple Gift of the Residue	1 copy
Will Form 2 - Residue to an Adult but if he/she dies to Children	1 copy
Will Form 3 - Residue Direct to Children	1 copy

For Scotland:

Will Form 1 - Simple Gift of the Residue	1 copy
Will Form 2 - Residue to an Adult but if he/she dies to Children	1 copy
Will Form 3 - Residue Direct to Children	1 copy

How to use this Kit

This Lawpack Kit can help you achieve an important legal objective conveniently, efficiently and economically. Nevertheless, it is important for you to use this Lawpack Kit properly if you are to avoid later difficulties.

- This Manual is divided into two parts: the first for those people making a Will who are domiciled in England, Wales, or Northern Ireland, and the second for those who are domiciled in Scotland. It is important that you use one of the Will Forms appropriate to where you are domiciled, as the law differs between jurisdictions. An explanation of domicile is given on page 6.

- Read carefully the parts of this Manual that are relevant to you. They contain the instructions you need to complete the England, Wales & Northern Ireland or Scotland Will Forms in this Lawpack Kit. If, after thorough examination, you decide that your requirements are not met by this Lawpack Kit, or you do not feel confident about writing your own documents, consult a solicitor.

- Refer to the completed examples and use the worksheets. When completing a Will Form, do not leave any section blank. If any section is inapplicable, write 'not applicable' or 'none.' This shows that you have not overlooked the section. If you do not fill the whole of one section, then put a line through the remaining blank space.

- Always use a pen or type on legal documents; never use pencil.

- If you cross out or erase anything on the final version of your Will Form you and your witnesses must sign in the margin against what is crossed out or erased.

- You will find a helpful glossary of terms at the end of each section of this Manual. Refer to the relevant glossary if you find unfamiliar terms.

- Once your Will is completed, you can, if you wish, photocopy and complete the additional documents at the end of this Manual that will be useful in the administration of your estate: Form of Letter to Executor, Funeral Wishes, Location of Important Documents, Important People to Notify and a Property Inventory.

- Do not amend the Will in any way once it has been witnessed – if you wish to change your Will, you should make a new one.

- Always keep legal documents in a safe place and in a location known to your spouse, family, executor or solicitor. Consider using Lawpack's Will Storage Service, details of which are contained in this Kit.

Downloads

This Kit provides access to free downloadable content, including electronic versions of the Will Forms and other documents. Please refer to the loose-flyer included in this Kit for information on how to access your downloads. Note that this Kit is fully functional without having to use the downloads.

Domicile

Consider whether the Will Forms for England, Wales & Northern Ireland or for Scotland are appropriate for you. It is important that you use the Will Forms applicable to where you are domiciled, because the law differs between the different jurisdictions.

Domicile is essentially – but not only – a question of where your permanent home is. If you have spent your whole life in one country and you consider that country to be your home, the position will be clear: that country will be your domicile. If you, or (when you were young) your parents, have moved countries, you should consider the paragraphs below in order to decide where your domicile is. If the situation is complex, or if you are in any way unsure, you should take legal advice.

At your birth you acquired a 'domicile of origin'. This is the domicile of your father if you were legitimate, or of your mother if you were not.

Your domicile may have changed later if two conditions were satisfied: first, that you resided in a different country; and second, you intended to reside there permanently or indefinitely. This is a 'domicile of choice'. Before you were 16, your domicile changed if – and only if – the domicile of your father, if you were legitimate, or your mother, if not, changed.

A domicile of choice may be abandoned if you no longer reside in the country and no longer intend to reside there permanently or indefinitely. If no new domicile of choice is acquired then the domicile of origin arises.

Making your Will in England, Wales & Northern Ireland

Why a Will is important

Without a valid Will you cannot control who will inherit your property after your death. Should you die intestate (without a Will), your property will be distributed according to law, which is likely to be inconsistent with your personal wishes. In some cases your estate may go to the Crown instead of the people you want to benefit. By making a Will you can determine precisely who will inherit your property and let your loved ones know that you have considered their needs.

Equally important, you can determine who will administer your estate and who will act as guardian for any minor children you have if they are left without a surviving parent. You can also use your Will to express your preferences for burial or cremation. In addition, making a Will gives you the opportunity of reducing your Inheritance Tax liability. This is particularly important if you have substantial assets.

When you die leaving a valid Will that appoints one or two executors who are still living at the time of your death, legal ownership of all of your property passes automatically to those executors. In order to prove that they have the right to deal with your property, they must apply for a legal document confirming their right to do so from the Probate Registry. This process is called 'obtaining probate'.

What is intestacy?

If you die without making a Will, or if your Will is invalid, you die intestate. The management of your estate is then placed in the hands of administrators who are appointed by the court and who are likely to be close members of your family. The administrators distribute your estate according to the rules of intestacy.

The rules are complex, but broadly speaking the bulk of your estate will go to your spouse (including a registered civil partner*) or, if none, to your children (whether or not they are adults) and, if none, to other blood relatives. The effect of the rules depends partly on the size of your estate. If your estate is large (currently more than £250,000 where there are children – even if they are adults – and £450,000 where there are none), less than you expect may go to your spouse. So it is always prudent to have a valid Will rather than rely on the intestacy rules.

It is also possible to die partially intestate. This occurs if you fail to deal with all of your property in your Will or if a particular beneficiary dies before you.

You should avoid intestacy if you make a valid Will in accordance with the instructions in this Lawpack Kit.

---

*Since 2005 it has been possible for same-sex partners to register their relationships, so becoming 'registered civil partners'. For many purposes, and for most of the rules related to Wills and intestacy, registered civil partners are treated in the same way as spouses.

Who should make a Will?

Every adult can and should make a Will. Minors, i.e. those under 18, generally cannot make a Will as they are not deemed competent. (Except in Northern Ireland, where a married minor or a minor who has been married may make a valid Will.)

The only qualifications necessary are that you are of legal age and of sound mind. If there is a history of mental disorder or if an illness may be affecting your judgement in any way, you should consult a qualified doctor just before preparing your Will. This will help establish your competence and will be useful should your Will be contested later on the grounds of mental incapacity.

If you are married, both you and your spouse should prepare Wills. This is true even if marital assets are primarily in the name of one spouse. Usually you will wish to name your spouse as your main beneficiary and include an alternative gift to take effect if he or she predeceases you. The same applies to registered civil partners.

If you are not married but are living with someone and you want that person to benefit from your estate, it is particularly important to make a Will. This is so because the rules of intestacy make *no provision* for unmarried partners (other than registered civil partners). If you were to die intestate, your partner would receive nothing from your estate.

How long is a Will valid?

Once prepared, your Will is valid until revoked, which may occur in one of four ways:

1   By destruction, combined with the intention to revoke.

2   By making a new Will that revokes the old Will. The Lawpack England, Wales & Northern Ireland Will Forms all contain the phrase, 'I revoke all previous wills and codicils' in order to do this and will revoke any previous Wills you have made.

3   By marriage or remarriage, unless your Will expressly states that it is made in contemplation of that forthcoming marriage.

4   By entering into a registered civil partnership, unless your Will expressly states that it is made in contemplation of that forthcoming registered civil partnership.

Except in one of the above circumstances, your Will remains valid for an unlimited period of time. Note that a divorce does not revoke a Will – but see opposite.

When is it necessary to prepare a new Will?

You may need to revise your Will for any number of reasons. Common occasions for reviewing a Will include:

- **Changes in the family** – a baby is born, a child becomes 18 (or perhaps some significant later age), or there is a death.

- **Marriage** – automatically revokes a previous Will, unless your Will expressly states that it is made in contemplation of that forthcoming marriage. It is always safer to prepare a new Will upon marrying.

- **Civil partnership** – registering a civil partnership has the same effect as marriage.
- **Divorce** – unlike marriage, a divorce does not revoke a previous Will. But if your former spouse is named as a beneficiary, then upon divorce he or she will cease to be a beneficiary or receive a gift unless your Will expressly provides that the gift should still take effect if you divorce. If your former spouse is named executor, then upon divorce he or she will no longer be allowed to act as executor or obtain probate of your Will. It is best to make a new Will whenever you get divorced.
- **Dissolution of a civil partnership** – the dissolution of a civil partnership has the same effect as a divorce.
- **Separation** – does not have the effect on a Will which a divorce has, so it is best to review the Will as soon as separation occurs.
- **Change in financial circumstances** – you may have recently acquired assets which you would like to give to particular beneficiaries, or perhaps due to hard times your estate may have become insufficient to provide for the legacies you have made.
- **Changes in taxation** – if your estate is large enough (or becomes large enough) to attract tax, new taxes or reliefs or changes in the rates may call for changes in your Will.
- **Going to live abroad** – it is normally desirable to make a Will in the country where you reside to simplify the administration of your estate. It may also be helpful if you need to establish a change of domicile. Local advice should be sought.

In any case, it is a good idea to review your Will at least every year, so that it is always up to date.

Preparing to make your Will

Before making your Will, consider carefully what you wish it to contain. The two principal decisions are: first, who should manage your property and distribute your property according to the terms of your Will (your executor) and second, how you wish your property (i.e. everything you own) to be distributed after your death.

Before you make your Will:

- List the assets you own.
- Decide who is to receive those assets.

Make an inventory of your property, whether in your name alone or owned jointly with others. In this Manual you will find a template Property Inventory form to help you. You can also download a copy of this form (see enclosed flyer).

Then decide how you wish that property to be distributed. You can make gifts of specific property to particular people, as well as gifts of sums of money to particular people. Items or money that you do not specifically allocate will form the 'residue' of your estate and you must decide who is to receive this.

If you make no provision in your Will for someone who is financially dependent on you, that person may have a claim against your estate. That can also apply to a person you are living with including, but not limited to, civil partners, spouses and children. Where this risk exists, you should always consult a solicitor to assist you in drafting your Will.

It is always best to draft your Will as simply as possible in plain English. Avoid the use of legal words and phrases if you do not understand precisely what they mean.

Executors and trustees

An executor is a person named in your Will as having the responsibility of managing your property after your death and distributing that property according to the terms of your Will. That person will have to collect in and preserve your assets, pay all relevant taxes and liabilities, obtain a grant of probate, sell those assets that need to be sold, and finally distribute your assets to your beneficiaries.

In some instances, money may not be paid directly to all your beneficiaries and may be held for their benefit. This is most common where the gift is to minor children or to someone pending their fulfilment of a condition, such as reaching a certain age. If this happens, the money will be paid to the person or persons you appoint as trustee. We recommend that you appoint the same person or persons as both executor and trustee and the Will Forms in this Kit have been drafted to this effect.

Trustees are then responsible for holding the monies and looking after them for the benefit of the beneficiaries. They are entrusted with investing the monies and generally safeguarding them. In some instances, they have the ability to distribute all or part of the monies to the beneficiaries or use them for their benefit if they think this is in the interest of the beneficiaries.

You must appoint at least one executor to carry out the instructions in your Will and it is usual to appoint two. Two executors should be appointed if the Will contains a gift to children, some of whom may be under 18 when you die. You should also appoint a replacement executor in case one of the named executors is, for any reason, unable to act.

The primary concern in selecting executors is that they should be reliable and trustworthy in carrying out your wishes. It is also desirable that at least one executor should know the beneficiaries personally. Often the best way is to appoint the person who stands to benefit most from your Will as one executor, and another relative or close friend as the second executor to assist or to take over should the first be unable to act. A person cannot act as executor while under 18.

The duties of an executor need not be difficult and your executor can use a solicitor to process the necessary probate forms. Always check with your proposed executors in advance to be certain that they are willing to act; a template letter to an executor is provided at the end of this Manual, or you can download a copy (see enclosed flyer for details).

Guardians

A guardian is someone appointed by you to act in your place as a parent and so is given both the responsibility of caring for and the powers to make decisions about your children (i.e. parental responsibility). Guardians are frequently appointed on the understanding that they will personally look after the children in the event of the parents' death. Nevertheless, this is not a requirement of being a guardian, as the guardian's task is to *make the decisions* about where the child lives, with whom, what school they go to and so on.

The guardian is often, but need not necessarily be, the same person as the executor and trustee (see above). Their responsibilities are different: an executor deals with and has responsibility for the financial arrangements, whereas a guardian makes decisions about the wellbeing of the children. If the guardian is not the same as the executor, he or she should be able to cooperate with the executor.

The appointment of a guardian is only effective if both parents (or all persons with parental responsibility) are no longer alive.

If you have minor children, you should name a guardian to care for them in the event of them being left without any parents. Since a guardian takes the place of a parent, you should choose someone who can offer the best care for your children, such as a close relative who is willing to accept the responsibility.

The guardian can be (but need not be) one of your executors. Always check with your proposed guardian in advance to be certain that he or she is willing to act.

There are complications if:

- you were not married to the other parent when the child was born;
- you and the other parent have already been or become (after the making of the Will) divorced from each other; or
- a court order already exists or is made in the future relating to where the child is to live or to parental responsibility for the child.

In these cases, we advise you to see a solicitor.

Beneficiaries

Adults

There is no particular complexity in making a gift to an adult, whether a specific gift or a gift of residue. England, Wales & Northern Ireland Will Form 1 provides a simple Will which would apply if all the beneficiaries are adult (i.e. over 18). It would apply, for example, if you wished to give the whole of your estate to your children where all of them are adult.

Minor children

Where you make a gift to children (whether adult or minors) consider whether you wish to name them (e.g. 'to my children James and Alexander') or to identify them as 'my children'. Naming them avoids confusion where, for example, you have step-children you wish to benefit (who might not be considered as 'your' children), but it does mean that any children born after the Will and before your death are excluded. If you have any illegitimate children, a gift to 'my children' will include them as 'children'; that form of gift is better avoided and it is better to make any gift to an illegitimate child by naming him or her. A reference to 'my children' in your Will will include any children adopted by you.

A child cannot own significant assets, such as shares or interests in land, and so is not capable of receiving them by a Will. If you do leave assets to a child who is under the age of 18 at your death, they will be held on trust for the child until he or she reaches the age of 18. The trustee will essentially hold money that belongs to that child and will have to give it to them on his or her 18th birthday. This does not give rise to particular complexities and causes no difficulties in cases of small gifts (e.g. a sum of £500 to a nephew).

It is though common for parents to want their child or children to not receive substantial assets until they are 18, and often older. It is common for any such gift to be conditional on the child reaching that age so that he or she is not automatically entitled to the money and so if he or she dies before that age, it will be divided between the other children. In England, Wales & Northern Ireland Will Forms 2 and 3 you are asked to state the age at which you want your children to inherit the capital as opposed to the income of the residue of your estate. The wording means that if any child does not reach the stated age, that child's share would go to their children or, if none, be divided between the other children. Common ages to choose are 18, 21 and 25. We recommend using the age of 18. There may be tax charges to apply if an age greater than 18 but less than 25 is chosen, although those charges are unlikely to be great. If you wish to consider an age over 25, we recommend seeing a solicitor before doing so.

Before the child attains the age you specify, your trustees will have the power to pay money out of capital for the child's maintenance (for example, his or her education) or to advance the capital of his or her inheritance, or to use the capital for the child's benefit, but only if they think there are good reasons for doing so. This discretion is expanded by the 'Trustees' powers' clauses at the end of England, Wales & Northern Ireland Will Forms 2 and 3.

While the child is under 18, the trustees also have discretion to use the income from the inheritance for the child's maintenance, education and benefit. In the England, Wales & Northern Ireland Will Forms in this Lawpack Kit, any child has the right to all the income from the inheritance after reaching 18, whether or not you specify a greater age for taking the capital outright.

Charity

It is also possible for your Will to contain a gift to charity. Any gift to charity is exempt from Inheritance Tax. The gift may be a specific amount of money (a 'legacy'), specific property or the whole or a share of your residue (see page 13).

If you make a gift to charity you should be careful to identify an existing charitable organisation rather than naming a general purpose or using a loose description of the charity, since in these cases the gift may fail or cause complexity for your executor(s). For example, rather than leaving £500 to 'cancer treatment' leave it to 'Cancer Research UK'.

Gifts

Specific gifts and legacies

You have the option of making specific gifts of individual items to named beneficiaries. Any asset you do not give as a specific gift and which is not used to pay debts, legacies, tax or the expenses of administering your estate is part of the 'residue' of your estate.

Consider any specific gift carefully. Are there family heirlooms that would have a special meaning to someone? Do you want to leave a particular item to a nephew, for example? If you are a mother, would you not prefer to leave your jewellery to your daughter? A specific gift may not necessarily have monetary importance, but may have personal significance.

In the case of specific gifts, always indicate clearly who is to receive each item of property. Give names in full and identify each item of property clearly. Try to avoid making gifts of property that are transitory in nature or which may have been sold or changed form before your death. Particular difficulties can arise with, for example, gifts of shares or bank accounts.

> **Examples of simple gifts:** 'I give my stamp collection to my son Alexander Guy Ross.'
> 'I give my Rolex watch to my son James Ross.'

Sometimes a particular item of property is charged with payment of a debt or other liability. The most common example is where a house is subject to a mortgage in favour of the bank. The widest term for such charges is 'encumbrances'. You should clearly indicate whether the person who receives the property takes it subject to the encumbrance, or free from the encumbrance, in which case the encumbrance will be paid out of the residue of the estate.

The following wording should be used for the gift of the property you live in at your death (a) subject to the payment of the mortgage and (b) not subject to such payment (so that the mortgage will be met by other assets in your estate):

(a) 'I give all my share and interest in my property at _____ subject to and charged with the payment of all principal sums and interest secured thereon by way of mortgage or otherwise at my death to _____ absolutely.'

(b) 'I give to _____ all my share and interest in my property at _____ absolutely freed and discharged from all sums secured thereon by way of mortgage or otherwise at my death and I direct that such sums and all interest in respect thereof shall be paid out of my residuary estate.'

It is also possible to make a gift of an amount of money in a Will. This is usually called a legacy. Again, you should clearly indicate the amount and the person who is to receive it.

Examples:
'I give to my son Alexander Guy Ross the sum of £100.'

'I give the sum of £100 to each of my grandchildren who shall be living as at the date of my death.'

'I give the sum of £1,000 to be divided equally between all my grandchildren who are living at the date of my death.'

'I give the sum of £1,000 to Macmillan Cancer Relief Fund.'

The residuary gift

The residuary gift or 'residue' is what is left of your estate after the deduction of specific gifts, debts, legacies, tax and the expenses of administration.

If you decide to make no specific gifts, but instead give all of your property to one beneficiary alone, then this gift becomes the 'residuary gift' and the beneficiary will receive whatever is left after the necessary deductions have been made.

You must make a residuary gift in your Will, otherwise you will die partially intestate. This means that any specific gifts and legacies can be distributed according to your wishes, but the remainder of your property, which makes up the residue, will be distributed under the rules of intestacy outlined above. This could result in a distribution you may not have wanted.

Your residuary gift can be given to any number of beneficiaries, but if it is given to more than one, you must state the share of the residue that each beneficiary is to receive, whether equal or otherwise.

A replacement residuary beneficiary

If a beneficiary to whom you have given a specific gift or legacy dies before you, that gift will pass instead to your residuary beneficiary.

If your residuary beneficiary dies before you, the gift cannot pass to anyone else and there will be a partial intestacy. It is wise, therefore, to name an alternative or replacement beneficiary who will take the residuary beneficiary's gift if he or she dies before you. Doing this avoids the possibility of partial intestacy and gives you greater control over the destiny of your property.

Although it is unlikely, it is also possible for a residuary beneficiary to die at the same time as you or very shortly after you, perhaps as a result of an accident affecting both of you. Your residue may pass to the residuary beneficiary and then almost immediately pass on, either under the beneficiary's Will or, if none, under the rules of intestacy, and again result in a distribution you may not have wanted. The inclusion of a survivorship clause prevents this process and allows you to decide who will inherit your property. The survivorship period can be up to six months but it is common to choose 28 days.

> **Example:** 'I give the residue of my estate to my wife Gillian Ross but if she fails to survive me by 28 days or if this gift fails for any reason, I give the residue to my brother Richard Ross.'

The survivorship clause by its nature also covers the event of the residuary beneficiary predeceasing you or dying in circumstances (such as a plane crash) where it is uncertain who died first.

The England, Wales & Northern Ireland Will Forms 1 and 2 contain survivorship clauses, but the England, Wales & Northern Ireland Will Form 3 (residue direct to children) does not.

If you give your residue initially to more than one person in shares, you need to make clear whether if one of them dies that person's share goes:

- to another person as replacement beneficiary, or
- to the survivors of the people you named initially.

In the England, Wales & Northern Ireland Will Form 1 the Residuary Gift reads:

> 'I GIVE the rest of my estate to my executors and trustees to hold on trust to pay my debts, taxes and testamentary expenses and pay the residue to _____ but if he/she or (if I have indicated more than one person) any of them fails to survive me by 28 days or if this gift or any part of it fails for any other reason, then I GIVE the residue of my estate or the part of it affected to _____ ,'

So if you name another person as replacement beneficiary and any of the persons named initially dies, his or her share will pass to the replacement beneficiary. However, if you have initially named more than one person, it is unlikely that all of them will fail to survive you. If you want the share of any who die to go to the others, you should write at the end of the Residuary Gift 'the other residuary beneficiary' if you initially named only two, or 'the other residuary beneficiaries in proportion to their shares' if you initially named more than two.

> **Example:** 'I GIVE the rest of my estate to my executors and trustees to hold on trust to pay my debts, taxes and testamentary expenses and pay the residue to David Peter Ross, Susanna Hill and Nigel Jones in equal shares but if he/she or (if I have indicated more than one person) any of them fails to survive me by 28 days or if this gift or any part of it fails for any other reason, then I GIVE the residue of my estate or the part of it affected to the other residuary beneficiaries in proportion to their shares'

In the England, Wales & Northern Ireland Will Form 2, if you name two or more adults to take initially and one dies, his or her share will go to your children.

If this is not what you want or any of the above is not clear, you should consult a solicitor.

Replacement gifts after gifts to children

In the case of gifts to children the position is different. In the England, Wales & Northern Ireland Will Forms 2 and 3 you are asked to state the age at which you want the children to inherit the capital of your estate. A child who is living at your death and has attained the stated age will inherit immediately. If living at your death, but not yet of the stated age, the child will inherit on reaching that age. Remember that a child can never hold property in his or her own name before the age of 18.

If a child of yours dies without leaving children, whether before you or after your death but under the stated age, the England, Wales & Northern Ireland Will Forms 2 and 3 will ensure that the share which the child would have taken will go to increase the shares of your other children.

If, on the other hand, a child of yours dies under the stated age leaving his or her own children (your grandchildren), different rules apply. The England, Wales & Northern Ireland Will Forms 2 and 3 make clear what is to happen with the following words:

'If any of my children dies before me or after me but under that age, I GIVE the share that child would have taken to his or her own children who attain 18 equally.'

If you do not want your grandchildren to inherit under these circumstances, you should see a solicitor. Do not simply delete the relevant words in the England, Wales & Northern Ireland Will Forms, because this will not have the effect you require.

It is also wise to see a solicitor if one of your children is no longer alive when you make your Will, but has left children who are still alive.

Disposal of property during your lifetime

People often believe that once they leave property under their Will they lose the right to sell or otherwise dispose of the property during their lifetime. This is not so. You retain the right to do whatever you choose with your property, notwithstanding its mention in your Will.

> **Example:** 'I give my house, 5 Maple Terrace, London, SW10 2PZ, to my friend Peter Harrison.'

means that your friend Peter only inherits 5 Maple Terrace if you own it at the time of your death. If you sold it and bought another house, your friend would not receive the new house in its place.

Obviously, if your Will includes many bequests that are no longer possible because you no longer possess the items, it is time to prepare a new Will to dispose of the assets you do have.

Property that does not pass under your Will

Joint tenancies

Is your home jointly owned with another person? If so, your share in the property may not pass under the terms of your Will and may automatically go to that other person. This depends upon whether the property is held under a 'joint tenancy' (where it will automatically go to that other person) or a 'tenancy in common' (where it will not).

A joint tenancy exists where you both own the whole property. A tenancy in common exists where you each own a specific share in the property. A tenancy in common must exist if you have defined your interests and those interests are not equal (i.e. two thirds/one third). However, the distinction between a joint tenancy and a tenancy in common is not easy where property is owned equally and if you are uncertain how your property is held, you should consult a solicitor.

Other property that is owned jointly may also be owned in what is in effect a joint tenancy. A particular example is bank accounts, which if in joint names are normally owned as joint tenancies.

If you wish to do so, you can (unless you are domiciled in Northern Ireland) easily change a joint tenancy into a tenancy in common by presenting your co-owner with written notice of your intention. It is important, however, that this written notice is given before your death, and not in your Will. If you wish to do this, you should see a solicitor. The enabling legislation has not been passed in Northern Ireland, so if you are domiciled there and you want to change a joint tenancy into a tenancy in common, you must seek the advice of a solicitor.

A surviving joint tenant is liable to pay any tax that may be due on inheriting your share of the jointly owned property, unless you specify otherwise. This does not apply to spouses or registered civil partners. If you do not wish the other joint tenant to pay this tax personally, you must include the following statement in your Will:

> 'I wish the burden of any tax due on my interest in property held under a joint tenancy to fall on my residuary estate.'

Other property

Property which is situated abroad (which for this purpose includes any other jurisdiction in the UK other than where you are domiciled) might not pass under your Will. You should consult a solicitor if you own or have an interest in property abroad.

Generally, life insurance policies that are expressed to be for the benefit of your spouse and/or children do not pass under your Will and therefore do not form part of your estate. The premiums paid on such a policy are not taxable if paid out of normal disposable income. The policy can be written in such a way that the proceeds are not taxable when you die. A life insurance policy is a good way to provide your family with the funds to meet any tax payable upon your death. Consult your life insurance company for more details.

Your pension rights may pass outside your Will in the same way. Your employer or pension provider should have more details. In many cases, you will be able to name the person who is to benefit from your pension rights, but only in a separate document, not in your Will.

Tax considerations in estate planning

The main tax charged upon estates is Inheritance Tax (IHT). This is a tax on all the assets held by you on your death (including joint property) as well as upon gifts made by you within seven years before your death. If those assets and gifts do not exceed the current sum of £325,000 (known as the 'nil rate band'), your estate will not pay any tax. After that sum, tax is charged at 40 per cent.

It is possible to word the provisions of a Will in a manner that will reduce the tax burden on your estate. Set out below is a simplified explanation of the tax issues facing your estate and some of the factors you should consider when drafting your Will. The explanation is for guidance only and cannot replace more detailed advice from an accountant or a solicitor. If the value of your estate substantially exceeds the nil rate band on which Inheritance Tax is not charged, you really should ask an accountant or a solicitor to advise you about any possible ways of reducing the burden of tax on your estate.

There are some exemptions from IHT. First, there is no charge on property that goes to your spouse (or registered civil partner) or to charity. Second, certain property such as business property (not including investment properties) and agricultural property are either exempt or charged at lower rates. In order to maximise those exemptions you should consider making specific gifts of business or agricultural property rather than including such property as part of the residue and ensuring that, so far as possible, those are gifts to persons other than your spouse or a charity (as such gifts are exempt anyway).

Prior to the pre-budget report on 9 October 2007 most other Will planning involved ensuring that two spouses (or civil partners) maximised the use of their nil rate bands. Following the pre-budget report, where a person leaves all their estate to their spouse the survivor will have twice the available nil rate band on their death. That means that such planning is unnecessary and indeed it is now better to leave property to a spouse than to maximise the nil rate band using vehicles such as trusts.

There are also steps you can take in your lifetime that can minimise the amount of tax you pay:

- Gifts made more than seven years before you die are not subject to IHT. Consider whether there is property that you can give away now.

- Gifts totalling up to £3,000 per annum, payable to any person, (however long the donor lives) are exempt whenever made.

- Gifts made from 'normal expenditure out of income', in other words gifts that can be said to be normal for the individual and are made solely from income are exempt whenever made.

- Gifts by parents to the parties to a marriage or civil partnership up to £5,000 are exempt.

- Gifts by a grandparent or remoter ancestor of either party up to £2,500 or gifts by any other person in consideration of marriage or civil partnership up to £1,000 are exempt gifts.

- Gifts paid to children or other family members in order to maintain them (where they are unable to do so themselves) or to pay for their education or training whilst in full-time education (an example would be the payment of a child's university fees) are exempt.

    In your lifetime, you should not make any gift of a large asset (such as your home) without seeking advice. Such a lifetime gift needs care because it could cause other taxes to become payable and might not be effective for saving IHT.

Witnesses to your Will

To ensure the validity of your Will, it is important to have it properly witnessed. You need two witnesses who should be over 18 and preferably neither very old nor hard to trace, in case a question should arise later concerning the validity of your Will. A blind person cannot witness a Will.

Warning: It is vital that the witnesses to your Will are neither beneficiaries under the Will nor the spouses of beneficiaries. If a beneficiary or his or her spouse does witness your Will, the beneficiary will lose the benefit of his or her gift, but the Will remains valid.

An executor (or a spouse of an executor) or a professional adviser, who may wish to charge for his or her services, can safely act as a witness unless he or she is also a beneficiary, in which case another witness must be found.

Signing your Will

You must sign your Will in the presence of the two witnesses and they must then both sign in your presence and in the presence of each other as witnesses to your signature. Neither you nor any witness should leave the room until your Will is both signed and witnessed, and you should all see each other sign.

Use your usual signature, write in ink and date your Will. Be sure that the witnesses complete their names, addresses and occupations in the space provided on the England, Wales & Northern Ireland Will Forms.

How to revise your Will

Never attempt to revise or change your Will by altering it. The way to revise an existing Will is to prepare a new Will. A new Will should contain a clause revoking all previous Wills. The Lawpack England, Wales & Northern Ireland Will Forms all contain a revocation clause. For safety, however, you should also physically destroy any former Will, and any copies, so that it cannot be mistaken for your most recent Will, but only after you have signed and witnessed your new Will.

Remember, you should not add words or provisions, nor should you change, delete, cross out or erase any part of your Will once it has been prepared. Do not staple, clip or attach any other document to your Will.

Safekeeping of your Will

After completion, your Will should be kept in a safe place either at home or lodged with a bank or solicitor. Do not staple, clip or attach any other documents to it. Make sure that your executors and a member of your family know of its whereabouts. It is sensible to keep a photocopy of your Will in case the original is accidentally lost or destroyed but it should be marked clearly as only a copy.

Your original Will may be deposited at the Probate Registry for those domiciled in England or Wales, or at the Probate & Matrimonial Office in Belfast for those domiciled in Northern Ireland. This has several advantages, the most important being that your Will is guaranteed to be held securely. Since your Will is recorded, no attempt can be made to administer your estate by bypassing your Will.

Alternatively, you can use Lawpack's Will Storage Service, details of which can be found on page 63.

Using the England, Wales & Northern Ireland Will Forms

You should now be ready to draft your Will.

Select the worksheet corresponding to the Will Form that is appropriate to your circumstances and requirements. This depends upon whom you wish to receive the residue of your estate:

England, Wales & Northern Ireland Will Form 1	Should be used if you want to give the residue of your estate to an adult, and provide for another adult to take instead if the first fails to survive you by 28 days. This Form may also be used to give your residue to a charity.
England, Wales & Northern Ireland Will Form 2	Should be used if you want to give the residue of your estate to an adult, and provide for your children to take instead in equal shares if the adult fails to survive you by 28 days.
England, Wales & Northern Ireland Will Form 3	Should be used if you want to give the residue of your estate to your children in equal shares in any event.

Using the worksheets, prepare a rough copy first. Make any necessary corrections. When you are satisfied with your final version complete the appropriate Will Form. Type it or write in ink. If you prefer, you can download Will Forms 1, 2 and 3 and the template documents included in this Kit. For further details see enclosed flyer. Once completed, follow precisely the correct procedure as to signature, dating and witnessing to validate your Last Will & Testament.

Glossary

administrator (or administratix if female) – a person appointed by the court to manage the estate of a deceased person when there is no executor.

adult – under English law, a person aged 18 or over.

beneficiary – a person who receives a gift under a Will. A beneficiary may also be a person who receives payment from a life insurance policy or a trust.

civil partnership – a partnership registered under the Civil Partnership Act 2004.

civil partners – persons who are registered as partners under the Civil Partnership Act 2004.

codicil – a document that modifies some provision of a Will but does not revoke it.

encumbrance – usually a mortgage or charge upon property securing the payment of a debt or other liability.

estate – all the property belonging to a person at death.

executor (or executrix, if female) – a person named in a Will to manage the deceased's estate.

guardian – a person with parental responsibility for a minor child.

Inheritance Tax – a tax imposed on a person's estate upon death and in some cases on gifts during the person's lifetime.

intestate – dying without leaving a valid Will.

joint property – property owned jointly with another person or persons.

legacy – usually a gift of money in a Will.

minor – under English law, a person under the age of 18.

obtaining probate – the process of proving the validity of a Will, and the executor's authority to manage the estate.

residuary beneficiary – a beneficiary who receives the residue of an estate or part of it.

replacement beneficiary – a person designated as a beneficiary if someone else predeceases you or fails to survive you for a specified period or to reach a specified age.

residuary gift – a gift of residue made in a Will.

residue – the remainder of an estate after the deduction of tax, debts, specific gifts, legacies and the expenses of administration.

specific gift – a gift of a particular item of property in a Will.

testator (or testatrix, if female) – a person who makes a Will.

trust – an arrangement under which a person or persons (the trustee or trustees) hold and manage property for the benefit of another person or persons (the trust beneficiary or beneficiaries).

Will – a legal document which sets out the wishes of the testator for the distribution of his or her estate and certain other matters after his or her death.

witness – a person who signs a Will to verify the testator's signature on it.

Example of completed England, Wales & Northern Ireland Will Form 1

Last Will & Testament

ENGLAND, WALES & NORTHERN IRELAND WILL FORM 1 – SIMPLE GIFT OF THE RESIDUE

PRINT NAME AND ADDRESS
THIS Last Will & Testament is made by me RICHARD BERNARD ROSS
of 28 STAPLEFORTH ROAD, LONDON SW6 4LJ

I REVOKE all previous wills and codicils.

EXECUTORS' NAMES AND ADDRESSES
I APPOINT as executors and trustees of my will

DAVID PETER ROSS and ANTHONY WILLIAMS
of 5 MAPLE TERRACE of 17 ST. GEORGE'S CRESCENT
LONDON SW10 2PZ READING RG7 9XY

REPLACEMENT EXECUTOR'S NAME AND ADDRESS
and should one or more of them fail to or be unable to act I APPOINT to fill any vacancy
GILLIAN ROSS
of 5 MAPLE TERRACE, LONDON SW10 2PZ

SPECIFIC GIFTS AND LEGACIES
I GIVE ALL MY SHARE AND INTEREST IN MY COTTAGE AT ST IVES CORNWALL SUBJECT TO AND CHARGED WITH THE PAYMENT OF ALL PRINCIPAL SUMS AND INTEREST SECURED THEREON BY WAY OF MORTGAGE OR OTHERWISE AT MY DEATH TO MY BROTHER DAVID PETER ROSS ABSOLUTELY.
TWO THOUSAND POUNDS TO MY FRIEND RAYMOND WILLIAMS.

Example of completed England, Wales & Northern Ireland Will Form 1 (cont.)

RESIDUARY GIFT I GIVE the rest of my estate to my executors and trustees to hold on trust to pay my debts, taxes and testamentary expenses and pay the residue to _____

DAVID PETER ROSS, SUSANNA HILL AND NIGEL JONES

IN EQUAL SHARES.

but if he/she or (if I have indicated more than one person) any of them fails to survive me by 28 days or if this gift or any part of it fails for any other reason, then I GIVE the residue of my estate or the part of it affected to

THE OTHER RESIDUARY BENEFICIARIES IN PROPORTION TO THEIR SHARES

FUNERAL WISHES I WISH my body to be ☑ buried   ☐ cremated   ☐ other instructions _____

AT ST. DUNSTAN'S OLD CHURCH, LONDON SW6

DATE SIGNED by the above-named testator in our presence on the

10TH day of OCTOBER 20 11

and then by us in the testator's presence

TESTATOR'S SIGNATURE SIGNED _[signature]_

WITNESSES' SIGNATURES NAMES AND ADDRESSES

SIGNED _[signature]_   SIGNED _[signature]_

MARY TUCKER   SIMON KNOX

of 14 RAVENSCROFT GARDENS   of 86 PRESTON SQUARE

LONDON N12 5TB   LONDON SW6

occupation TEACHER   occupation COMPUTER CONSULTANT

Last Will & Testament

ENGLAND, WALES & NORTHERN IRELAND WILL FORM 1 – SIMPLE GIFT OF THE RESIDUE

PRINT NAME AND ADDRESS

THIS Last Will & Testament is made by me _____

of _____

I REVOKE all previous wills and codicils.

EXECUTORS' NAMES AND ADDRESSES

I APPOINT as executors and trustees of my will

_____ and _____

of _____ of _____

_____ _____

REPLACEMENT EXECUTOR'S NAME AND ADDRESS

and should one or more of them fail to or be unable to act I APPOINT to fill any vacancy

_____

of _____

SPECIFIC GIFTS AND LEGACIES

I GIVE _____

_____

_____

_____

_____

_____

_____

_____

_____

_____

_____

_____

_____

_____

_____

_____

_____

_____

RESIDUARY GIFT I GIVE the rest of my estate to my executors and trustees to hold on trust to pay my debts, taxes and testamentary expenses and pay the residue to _____

_____

_____

but if he/she or (if I have indicated more than one person) any of them fails to survive me by 28 days or if this gift or any part of it fails for any other reason, then I GIVE the residue of my estate or the part of it affected to

_____

FUNERAL WISHES I WISH my body to be ☐ buried ☐ cremated ☐ other instructions _____

_____

SIGNED by the above-named testator in our presence on the

DATE _____ day of _____ 20 _____

and then by us in the testator's presence

TESTATOR'S SIGNATURE SIGNED _____

WITNESSES' SIGNATURES NAMES AND ADDRESSES

SIGNED _____ SIGNED _____

_____ _____

of _____ of _____

_____ _____

occupation _____ occupation _____

Example of completed England, Wales & Northern Ireland Will Form 2

Last Will & Testament

ENGLAND, WALES & NORTHERN IRELAND WILL FORM 2 - RESIDUE TO AN ADULT BUT IF HE/SHE DIES TO CHILDREN

PRINT NAME AND ADDRESS

THIS Last Will & Testament is made by me GILLIAN ROSS

of 5 MAPLE TERRACE, LONDON SW10 2PZ

I REVOKE all previous wills and codicils.

EXECUTORS' NAMES AND ADDRESSES

I APPOINT as executors and trustees of my will

DAVID PETER ROSS   and   THERESA MUNDY

of 5 MAPLE TERRACE   of 9 KINGS WALK

LONDON SW10 2PZ   LEAMINGTON SPA LM9 4BL

REPLACEMENT EXECUTOR'S NAME AND ADDRESS

and should one or more of them fail to or be unable to act I APPOINT to fill any vacancy

THOMAS WAITE

of 36 AMBER ROAD, LONDON SW3 5MM

GUARDIAN'S NAME AND ADDRESS

I APPOINT THERESA MUNDY

of 9 KINGS WALK, LEAMINGTON SPA LM9 4BL

to be guardian of any of my children who are minors if my husband/wife dies before me.

SPECIFIC GIFTS AND LEGACIES

I GIVE ALL MY JEWELLERY TO MY DAUGHTER MARY JANE ROSS.

£5,000 TO EACH OF MY SONS, JAMES THOMAS ROSS AND

ALEXANDER GUY ROSS.

MY MOTOR CAR, REGISTRATION NUMBER T488 YVV, TO MY

FRIEND PETER HARRISON.

Example of completed England, Wales & Northern Ireland Will Form 2 (cont.)

RESIDUARY GIFT   I GIVE the rest of my estate to my executors and trustees to hold on trust to pay my debts, taxes and testamentary expenses and pay the residue to

MY HUSBAND DAVID PETER ROSS

(insert age at which you want your children to inherit capital)   but if he/she or (if I have indicated more than one person) any of them fails to survive me by 28 days or if this gift or any part of it fails for any other reason, then I GIVE the residue of my estate or the part of it affected to those of my children who survive me and attain the age of __21__ years if more than one in equal shares.

PROVIDED THAT if any of my children dies before me or after me but under that age, I GIVE the share that child would have taken to his or her own children who attain 18 equally. If no person shall inherit the residue of my estate or part of it under the preceding gifts, I GIVE it to

THERESA MUNDY

TRUSTEES' POWERS   My trustees shall have the power to apply for the benefit of any beneficiary as my trustees shall in their absolute discretion think fit the whole or any part of the capital to which such beneficiary is or may in the future be entitled.

FUNERAL WISHES   I WISH my body to be   ☐ buried   ☑ cremated   ☐ other instructions _____

DATE   SIGNED by the above-named testator in our presence on the

__10TH__ day of __OCTOBER__ 20 __11__

and then by us in the testator's presence

TESTATOR'S SIGNATURE   SIGNED _Gillian Ross_

WITNESSES' SIGNATURES NAMES AND ADDRESSES

SIGNED _Ruth Grant_   SIGNED _Jane Paxford_

RUTH GRANT   JANE PAXFORD

of __90 DORSET MANSIONS__   of __32 CHURCH GROVE__

__LONDON W14 2BS__   __LONDON SW6 6RQ__

occupation __HOUSEWIFE__   occupation __RECEPTIONIST__

Last Will & Testament

ENGLAND, WALES & NORTHERN IRELAND WILL FORM 2 - RESIDUE TO AN ADULT BUT IF HE/SHE DIES TO CHILDREN

PRINT NAME AND ADDRESS

THIS Last Will & Testament is made by me _____

of _____

I REVOKE all previous wills and codicils.

EXECUTORS' NAMES AND ADDRESSES

I APPOINT as executors and trustees of my will

_____ and _____

of _____ of _____

_____ _____

REPLACEMENT EXECUTOR'S NAME AND ADDRESS

and should one or more of them fail to or be unable to act I APPOINT to fill any vacancy

_____

of _____

GUARDIAN'S NAME AND ADDRESS

I APPOINT _____

of _____

to be guardian of any of my children who are minors if my husband/wife dies before me.

SPECIFIC GIFTS AND LEGACIES

I GIVE _____

_____
_____
_____
_____
_____
_____
_____
_____
_____
_____
_____
_____
_____
_____

RESIDUARY GIFT   I GIVE the rest of my estate to my executors and trustees to hold on trust to pay my debts, taxes and testamentary expenses and pay the residue to

_____

(insert age at which you want your children to inherit capital)   but if he/she or (if I have indicated more than one person) any of them fails to survive me by 28 days or if this gift or any part of it fails for any other reason, then I GIVE the residue of my estate or the part of it affected to those of my children who survive me and attain the age of _____ years if more than one in equal shares.

PROVIDED THAT if any of my children dies before me or after me but under that age, I GIVE the share that child would have taken to his or her own children who attain 18 equally. If no person shall inherit the residue of my estate or part of it under the preceding gifts, I GIVE it to

_____

TRUSTEES' POWERS   My trustees shall have the power to apply for the benefit of any beneficiary as my trustees shall in their absolute discretion think fit the whole or any part of the capital to which such beneficiary is or may in the future be entitled.

FUNERAL WISHES   I WISH my body to be   ☐ buried   ☐ cremated   ☐ other instructions _____

_____

DATE   SIGNED by the above-named testator in our presence on the

_____ day of _____ 20 _____

and then by us in the testator's presence

TESTATOR'S SIGNATURE   SIGNED _____

WITNESSES' SIGNATURES NAMES AND ADDRESSES   SIGNED _____   SIGNED _____

_____   _____

of _____   of _____

_____   _____

occupation _____   occupation _____

Example of completed England, Wales & Northern Ireland Will Form 3

Last Will & Testament

ENGLAND, WALES & NORTHERN IRELAND WILL FORM 3 - RESIDUE DIRECT TO CHILDREN

PRINT NAME AND ADDRESS

THIS Last Will & Testament is made by me GILLIAN ROSS

of 5 MAPLE TERRACE, LONDON SW10 2PZ

I REVOKE all previous wills and codicils.

EXECUTORS' NAMES AND ADDRESSES

I APPOINT as executors and trustees of my will

DAVID PETER ROSS and THERESA MUNDY

of 5 MAPLE TERRACE of 9 KINGS WALK

LONDON SW10 2PZ LEAMINGTON SPA LM9 4BL

REPLACEMENT EXECUTOR'S NAME AND ADDRESS

and should one or more of them fail to or be unable to act I APPOINT to fill any vacancy

THOMAS WAITE

of 36 AMBER ROAD, LONDON SW3 5MM

GUARDIAN'S NAME AND ADDRESS

I APPOINT THERESA MUNDY

of 9 KINGS WALK, LEAMINGTON SPA LM9 4BL

to be guardian of any of my children who are minors if my husband/wife dies before me.

SPECIFIC GIFTS AND LEGACIES

I GIVE ALL OF MY JEWELLERY TO MY DAUGHTER MARY JANE ROSS. £10,000 TO EACH OF MY SONS, JAMES ROSS AND ALEXANDER GUY ROSS. ALL MY SHARE AND INTEREST IN MY HOUSE AT 5 MAPLE TERRACE LONDON SW10 2PZ SUBJECT TO AND CHARGED WITH THE PAYMENT OF ALL PRINCIPAL SUMS AND INTEREST SECURED THEREON BY WAY OF MORTGAGE OR OTHERWISE AT MY DEATH TO MY HUSBAND DAVID PETER ROSS ABSOLUTELY.

Example of completed England, Wales & Northern Ireland Will Form 3 (cont.)

RESIDUARY GIFT
(insert age at which you want your children to inherit capital)

I GIVE the rest of my estate to my executors and trustees to hold on trust to pay my debts, taxes and testamentary expenses and pay the residue to those of my children who survive me and attain the age of __21__ years if more than one in equal shares.

PROVIDED THAT if any of my children dies before me or after me but under that age, I GIVE the share that child would have taken to his or her own children who attain 18 equally. If no person shall inherit the residue of my estate under the preceding gifts, I GIVE it to _____

THERESA MUNDY

TRUSTEES' POWERS

My trustees shall have the power to apply for the benefit of any beneficiary as my trustees shall in their absolute discretion think fit the whole or any part of the capital to which such beneficiary is or may in the future be entitled.

FUNERAL WISHES

I WISH my body to be   ☐ buried   ☑ cremated   ☐ other instructions _____

DATE

SIGNED by the above-named testator in our presence on the __10TH__ day of __OCTOBER__ 20 __11__

and then by us in the testator's presence

TESTATOR'S SIGNATURE

SIGNED _Gillian Ross_

WITNESSES' SIGNATURES NAMES AND ADDRESSES

SIGNED _Ruth Grant_   SIGNED _Jane Paxford_

RUTH GRANT   JANE PAXFORD

of 90 DORSET MANSIONS   of 32 CHURCH GROVE

LONDON W14 2BS   LONDON SW6 6RQ

occupation HOUSEWIFE   occupation RECEPTIONIST

Last Will & Testament

ENGLAND, WALES & NORTHERN IRELAND WILL FORM 3 - RESIDUE DIRECT TO CHILDREN

PRINT NAME AND ADDRESS
THIS Last Will & Testament is made by me _____
of _____

I REVOKE all previous wills and codicils.

EXECUTORS' NAMES AND ADDRESSES
I APPOINT as executors and trustees of my will
_____ and _____
of _____ of _____
_____ _____

REPLACEMENT EXECUTOR'S NAME AND ADDRESS
and should one or more of them fail to or be unable to act I APPOINT to fill any vacancy
_____
of _____

GUARDIAN'S NAME AND ADDRESS
I APPOINT _____
of _____
to be guardian of any of my children who are minors if my husband/wife dies before me.

SPECIFIC GIFTS AND LEGACIES
I GIVE _____
_____
_____
_____
_____
_____
_____
_____
_____
_____
_____
_____
_____
_____
_____

RESIDUARY GIFT
(insert age at which you want your children to inherit capital)

I GIVE the rest of my estate to my executors and trustees to hold on trust to pay my debts, taxes and testamentary expenses and pay the residue to those of my children who survive me and attain the age of _____ years if more than one in equal shares.

PROVIDED THAT if any of my children dies before me or after me but under that age, I GIVE the share that child would have taken to his or her own children who attain 18 equally. If no person shall inherit the residue of my estate under the preceding gifts, I GIVE it to _____

_____

TRUSTEES' POWERS

My trustees shall have the power to apply for the benefit of any beneficiary as my trustees shall in their absolute discretion think fit the whole or any part of the capital to which such beneficiary is or may in the future be entitled.

FUNERAL WISHES

I WISH my body to be ☐ buried ☐ cremated ☐ other instructions _____

_____

DATE

SIGNED by the above-named testator in our presence on the

_____ day of _____ 20 _____

and then by us in the testator's presence

TESTATOR'S SIGNATURE

SIGNED _____

WITNESSES' SIGNATURES NAMES AND ADDRESSES

SIGNED _____   SIGNED _____

_____   _____

of _____   of _____

_____   _____

occupation _____   occupation _____

Making your Will in Scotland

Why a Will is important

Without a valid Will you cannot control who will inherit your property after your death. Should you die intestate (without a Will), your property will be distributed according to law, which is likely to be inconsistent with your personal wishes. In some cases your estate may go to the Crown instead of the people you want to benefit. By making a Will you can determine precisely who will inherit your property and let your loved ones know that you have considered their needs.

Equally important, you can determine who will administer your estate and who will act as guardian for any minor children you have if they are left without a surviving parent. You can also use your Will to express your preferences for burial or cremation and for donating organs or your entire body for medical purposes. In addition, making a Will gives you the opportunity of reducing the Inheritance Tax liability of your estate. This is particularly important if you have substantial assets.

When you die, your property must be gathered in and distributed to your beneficiaries. Your executors are responsible for this task and they are appointed either by you in your Will (Executor Nominate), or by the Sheriff Court (Executor Dative). Before your executors can uplift (secure the release of) and deal with your assets they must normally obtain 'Confirmation'. Confirmation is granted by the Sheriff, and gives the executors authority to administer the estate.

What is intestacy?

If you die without making a Will, or if your Will is invalid, you die intestate. The management of your estate is then placed in the hands of executors who are appointed by the court and who are likely to be close members of your family. The executors distribute your estate according to the rules of intestacy.

The rules are complex but, broadly speaking, the bulk of your estate will go to your spouse or civil partner* (but not necessarily wholly, whether or not you have children) or to your children and, if none, to other members of the family. The effect of the rules depends partly on the size of your estate. If your estate is large, less than you expect may go to your spouse or civil partner.

It is also possible to die partially intestate. This occurs if you fail to deal with all of your property in your Will or if a particular beneficiary dies before you. You should avoid intestacy if you make a valid Will in accordance with the instructions in this Lawpack Kit.

Who should make a Will?

Every adult can and should make a Will. Children under the age of 12 cannot make a Will as they are not deemed competent.

---

*Since 2005 it has been possible for same-sex partners to register their relationships so becoming 'civil partners'. For many purposes, and for most of the rules relating to Wills and intestacy, civil partners are treated in the same way as spouses.

The only qualifications necessary are that you are over 12 and of sound mind. If there is a history of mental disorder or if an illness may be affecting your judgement in any way, you should consult a qualified doctor just before preparing your Will. This will help establish your competence and will be useful should your Will be contested later on the grounds of mental incapacity.

If you are married or in a civil partnership, both you and your spouse or civil partner should prepare Wills. This is true even if marital assets are primarily in the name of one spouse or one civil partner. Usually you will wish to name your spouse or civil partner as your main beneficiary and include a replacement gift to take effect if he or she predeceases you.

If you are not married and not in a civil partnership but are living with someone and you want that person to benefit from your estate, it is particularly important to make a Will. This is so because the rules of intestacy make no provision for unmarried partners (other than civil partners). If you were to die intestate, your partner (if not a civil partner) may receive nothing from your estate. The Family Law (Scotland) Act 2006 allows a cohabitant of a person who dies intestate to apply to the court for payment out of the deceased's net estate of a capital sum or for the transfer to the surviving cohabitant of the deceased's property, which can include a house. The court has to take into account the size and nature of the deceased's net intestate estate, any benefit being received by the surviving cohabitant on, or as a consequence of the deceased's death (e.g. being paid out from a Life Policy), any benefits received other than from the deceased's net intestate estate and the nature and extent of any other claims on the deceased's estate e.g. from children. The maximum the court can award is the same as the cohabitant would have received if they had been married or a civil partner of the deceased. Any award made by the court is at the discretion of the court and accordingly if you wish to ensure that your unmarried partner is provided for, you would be best to make a Will.

How long is a Will valid?

Once prepared, your Will is valid until revoked, which may occur in one of three ways:

1. By destruction, combined with the intention to revoke.
2. By making a new Will that revokes the old Will, by use of the phrase, 'I revoke all previous wills and codicils'. The Lawpack Scotland Will Forms all contain this revocation clause. If you have made a separate Will dealing with property abroad, you should consult a solicitor.
3. Probably if you have a child, after having made your Will, where the Will makes no provision for that child. The law presumes that you would wish to provide for your child in your Will, and therefore if no mention of the child is made in your Will, the law presumes (which presumption would be difficult to overcome or rebut) that because the child is disadvantaged by not being provided for, the Will is revoked.

Other than in one of these circumstances, your Will remains valid for an unlimited period of time.

Note that marriage, civil partnership, divorce and remarriage do not revoke a Will.

When is it necessary to prepare a new Will?

You may need to revise your Will for any number of reasons. Common occasions for revising a Will include:

- **Change in financial circumstances** – you may have recently acquired assets which you would like to give to particular beneficiaries, or perhaps due to hard times your estate may have become insufficient to provide for the legacies you have made.

- **Marriage or civil partnership** – does not revoke a previous Will, but you may well wish to make a new Will to provide for your new family.
- **Family additions** – the birth of a child may necessitate a new Will as your existing Will may not provide for this child. (See 'How long is a Will valid?')
- **Changes in taxation** – if your estate is large enough (or becomes large enough) to attract tax, new taxes, reliefs or changes in the rates may call for changes in your Will.
- **Going to live abroad** – it is normally desirable to make a Will in the country where you reside to simplify the administration of your estate. It may also be helpful if you need to establish a change of domicile. Local advice should be sought.
- **Divorce** – does not revoke a previous Will. For this reason, great care must be taken when using the words 'husband' or 'wife' in a Will, because when used alone, the word will 'speak from your death', which means the gift will go to whomever is your husband or wife at the time of your death. In this case, an earlier spouse would lose his or her gift to a later spouse, possibly contrary to your intention. For the avoidance of doubt, always identify your spouse by name when making your Will, e.g. 'my wife, Gillian', and draw up a new Will on separation or divorce. Divorce is a complex issue and we recommend you consult a solicitor if in doubt.
- **Dissolution of a civil partnership** – the dissolution of a civil partnership has the same effect as a divorce.

In any case, it is a good idea to review your Will from time to time and in any event not less often than every five years, so that it is always up to date.

Preparing to make your Will

Before making your Will consider carefully what you wish it to contain. The two principal decisions are: first, who should manage your property and distribute your property according to the terms of your Will (the executor) and second, how you wish your property to be distributed after your death.

Before you make your Will:

- List the assets you own.
- Decide who is to receive those assets.

Make an inventory of everything you own, whether in your name alone or jointly with others. In this Manual you will find a template Property Inventory to help you. You can also download a copy of this form (see enclosed flyer for further details).

Then decide how you wish that property to be distributed. You can make gifts of specific property to particular people as well as gifts of sums of money to particular people. Items or money that you do not specifically allocate will form the 'residue' of your estate and you must decide who is to receive this.

Whether or not you make a Will, your spouse, or civil partner and issue are entitled to claim 'legal rights' which enable your surviving spouse or civil partner and surviving children (and surviving issue of predeceasing children) to claim part of your estate at death as an alternative to (but not in addition to) the benefits that you might have provided for them in your Will. In effect, these legal rights protect your spouse or civil partner and issue against getting little or nothing from your estate. Such legal rights cannot be overruled by a Will. These legal rights are (a) in the case of a surviving spouse or civil partner where your children (or remoter issue) survive, one third of your 'moveable estate' (i.e. all your estate other than land and buildings), and where you leave no surviving children (or surviving remoter issue), one half of your moveable estate and (b) in the case of surviving children (and surviving issue of predeceasing children) where there is a surviving spouse or civil partner, one third of your moveable estate and where there is no surviving spouse or civil partner, one half of your moveable estate.

It is always best to draft your Will as simply as possible in plain English. Avoid the use of legal words and phrases if you do not understand precisely what they mean.

Executors and trustees

An executor is a person named in your Will as having the responsibility of managing your property after your death and distributing that property according to the terms of your Will. That person will have to collect in and preserve your assets, pay all relevant taxes and liabilities, obtain a grant of Confirmation, sell those assets that need to be sold and finally distribute your assets to your beneficiaries.

In some instances money may not be paid directly to all your beneficiaries and may be held for their benefit. This is most common where the gift is to minor children or to someone pending their fulfilling a condition such as reaching a certain age. If this happens, the money will be paid to the person or persons you appoint as trustee. We recommend that you appoint the same person or persons as both executor and trustee and the Will Forms have been drafted to this effect.

Trustees are then responsible for holding the monies and looking after them for the benefit of the beneficiaries. They are entrusted with investing the monies and generally safeguarding them. In some instances, they have the ability to distribute all or part of it to the beneficiaries or use it for their benefit if they think this is in the interest of the beneficiaries.

You must appoint at least one executor to carry out the instructions in your Will and it is recommended that you appoint two, particularly if you have provided for underage beneficiaries. You should also appoint a replacement executor in case one of the named executors is, for any reason, unable to act.

The primary concern in selecting executors is that they should be reliable and trustworthy in carrying out your wishes. It is also desirable that at least one executor should know the beneficiaries personally. Your executors will also be the trustees of any trust you set up for your children (see 'Underage children'). Often it is best to appoint the person who stands to benefit most from your Will as one executor and another person with no financial interest in the estate, but who knows the family, as the second executor, to assist or to take over should the first be unable to act. Age is no disqualification to becoming an executor. However, it is recommended that only persons over the age of 16 are appointed.

The duties of an executor need not be difficult and will involve processing certain forms to obtain Confirmation, and any forms required once Confirmation has been received. You do not need to check with your proposed executors in advance that they would be willing to act (you may always change your Will or you may not want to disclose to anyone what provisions you are making in your Will), unless you have a doubt as to whether they would be willing to act; a form of letter to a proposed executor is provided in this Manual, if deemed appropriate, or you can download a copy (see enclosed flyer for further details).

Guardians

A guardian is someone appointed by you to act in your place as a parent and so is given the responsibility of caring for, and the powers to make decisions about, your children (i.e. parental responsibility). Guardians are frequently appointed on the understanding that they will personally look after the children in the event of the parents' death. Nevertheless, this is not a requirement of being a guardian as the guardian's task is to make the decisions about where the child lives, with whom, what school they go to and so on.

The guardian is often, but need not necessarily be the same person as the executor and trustee (see above). Their responsibilities are different – an executor deals with and has responsibility for the financial arrangements whereas a guardian makes decisions about the wellbeing of the children. If the guardian is not the same as the executor, he or she should be able to co-operate with the executor.

The appointment of a guardian is only effective if both parents (or all persons with parental responsibility) are no longer alive.

If you have underage children (i.e. under the age of 16), you should name a guardian to care for them in the event that they are left without a parent. Since a guardian takes the place of a parent, you should choose someone who can offer the best care for your children, such as a close relative, who is willing to accept the responsibility. The guardian can be (but need not be) one of your executors. The appointment of a guardian must be in writing and signed by a parent. This rule is satisfied if you include the appointment in your Will by completing the relevant section in the Scotland Will Form. However, it should be noted that any appointment of a guardian is not binding on a court, if the matter is disputed.

There are complications if:

- you were not married to the other parent when the child was born;
- you and the other parent have already been or become (after the making of the Will) divorced from each other; or
- a court order already exists or is made in the future relating to where the child is to live or to parental responsibility for the child.

In these cases we advise you to see a solicitor.

Beneficiaries

Adults

There is no particular complexity in making a gift to an adult, whether a specific gift or a gift of residue. Scotland Will Form 1 provides a simple Will Form which would apply if all the beneficiaries are adult (i.e. over 16). It would apply, for example, if you wished to give the whole of your estate to your children where all of them are adult.

Underage children

A child under 16 has no legal capacity to administer property that is left to him or her under a Will. The property will instead be held on trust for the child until the age of 16 (or a later age if specified) by your executors as trustees (unless you provide for your executors to pay or make over the property to the guardian of the child concerned). You should bear in mind that if the executor is not the parent or guardian of the child and you provide for the executor to pay over property to the parent or guardian of a child under 16 and that sum exceeds £20,000 there is an obligation in terms of the Children (Scotland) Act 1995 for the executor to apply to the accountant of the court for a direction as to the administration of the property. If the value of the property is between £5,000 to £20,000 the executor may apply to the accountant of the court, although there is no obligation to do so. You are therefore asked in Scotland Will Forms 2 and 3 to state the age at which you want your children to inherit the 'capital' as opposed to the 'income' of your estate. Common ages to choose are 18, 21 and 25. The Scotland Will Forms also allow you to state the age at which you wish your children to receive the right to the income. Arising from the provisions of the Finance Act 2006, if the age selected for children to inherit were beyond 18 years, in cases where the estate passing to such children exceeds the threshold for payment of Inheritance Tax (£325,000 for 2009/10 and 2010/11), then on the children inheriting, an Inheritance Tax charge on the excess over the threshold (albeit limited) would arise.

The Scotland Will Forms ensure that the funds are not completely locked up until the age you choose. Before the child attains the age you specify, your trustees will have the power to advance the capital of his or her inheritance, or to use the capital for the child's benefit, but only if they think there are good reasons for doing so.

Also, while the child is under the age at which you state he or she can claim income from the inheritance, the trustees will have discretion to use the income for the child's maintenance, education and benefit; or to accumulate the income by adding it to the capital. There are certain restricted periods of accumulation of income.

Where you make a gift to children (whether adult or underage) consider whether you wish to name them (e.g. 'to my children James and Alexander') or to identify them as 'my children'. Naming them avoids confusion where, for example, you have step-children you wish to benefit (who might not be considered as your children) but it does mean that any children born after the Will and before your death are excluded. If you have any children from a previous relationship, a gift to 'my children' will include them as children; that form of gift is better avoided and it is better to make any gift to a child of a previous relationship by naming him or her.

Charity

It is also possible for your Will to contain a gift to charity. Any gift to charity is exempt from Inheritance Tax. The gift may be of a specific amount of money (legacy) specific property or of the whole or a share of your residue (see page 38).

If you make a gift to charity, you should be careful to identify an existing charitable organisation rather than naming a general purpose or using a loose description of the charity since in these cases the gift may fail or even go to 'the wrong charity' or cause complexity for your executor. For example, rather than leaving £500 to 'cancer treatment' leave it to 'Cancer Research UK'.

Gifts

Specific gifts and legacies

You have the option of making specific gifts of individual items to named beneficiaries. Any asset you do not give as a specific gift and which is not used to pay debts, legacies, any legal rights payments, tax or the expenses of administering your estate is part of the residue of your estate.

Consider any specific gift carefully. Are there family heirlooms that would have a special meaning to someone? Do you want to leave a particular item to a nephew, for example? If you are a mother, would you not prefer to leave your jewellery to your daughter? A specific gift may not necessarily have monetary importance but may have personal significance.

If you leave specific items to your children or nephews or nieces (unless the Will makes it clear otherwise), the law assumes that if he or she dies before you, leaving children or remoter descendants of his or her own who survive you, then you wish the descendants to receive the legacy in his or her place. If this is not what you wish to happen, you should add:

'But expressly excluding the issue of [insert name] in the event of his/her or their failing to survive me.'

In the case of specific gifts, always indicate clearly who is to receive each item of property. Give names and addresses in full and identify each item of property clearly. Try to avoid making gifts of property that are transitory in nature or which may have been sold or changed form before you die. Particular difficulties can arise with, for example, gifts of shares or bank accounts.

> **Examples:** 'I give my stamp collection to my son Alexander Guy Ross.'
> 'I give my Rolex watch to my son James Ross.'

It is also possible to make a gift of an amount of money in a Will. This is usually called a 'pecuniary legacy'. The provision that all pecuniary legacies are to be paid free of interest is included in a statement in the Will Forms. Again, you should clearly indicate the amount and the person who is to receive it.

> **Examples:** 'I give to my son Alexander Guy Ross the sum of £100.'
> 'I give the sum of £100 to each of my grandchildren who shall be in life at the date of my death.'
> 'I give the sum of £1,000 to be divided equally between or among such of my grandchildren who shall be in life at the date of my death.'

Sometimes a particular item of property is charged with payment of a debt or other liability. The most common example is where a house is subject to a mortgage in favour of a bank or building society. The widest term for such charges is 'encumbrances'. You should clearly indicate whether the person who receives the property takes it subject to the encumbrance, or free from the encumbrance, in which case the encumbrance will be paid out of the residue of estate.

The following wording should be used for the gift of the property you live in at your death, (a) subject to the payment of the mortgage, or (b) not subject to such payment (so that the mortgage will be met by other assets in your estate):

> (a) 'I give my house (or my whole interest therein) at_____ to _____ residing at _____ subject to any existing mortgage on it.'
>
> (b) 'I give my house (or my whole interest therein) at_____ to _____ residing at _____ free from any mortgage (any mortgage being repaid out of the residue of my estate).'

The residuary gift

The residue is the term used to describe what is left of your estate after the deduction of tax, debts, specific gifts, pecuniary legacies, any legal rights payments and the expenses of administering the estate.

If you decide to make no specific gifts, but instead to give all of your property to one beneficiary alone, then this gift becomes the 'residuary gift', and the beneficiary will receive whatever is left of your estate after the necessary deductions have been made.

You must make a residuary gift in your Will, otherwise you will die partially intestate. This means that any specific gifts and pecuniary legacies can be distributed according to your wishes, but the remainder of your property, which makes up the residue, will be distributed under the rules of intestacy outlined under 'What is intestacy?' on page 32. This could result in a property distribution you may not have wanted.

Your residuary gift can be given to any number of beneficiaries, but if it is given to more than one, you must state the share of the residue that each beneficiary is to receive, whether equal or otherwise.

A replacement residuary beneficiary

If a beneficiary to whom you have given a specific gift or legacy dies before you, that gift will pass instead to your residuary beneficiary.

If your residuary beneficiary dies before you, the gift cannot pass to anyone else and there will be a partial intestacy unless the beneficiary was your child, grandchild or remoter direct descendant (or your niece or nephew). It is wise, therefore, to name an alternative or replacement beneficiary who will take the residuary beneficiary's gift if he or she dies before you. Doing this avoids the possibility of partial intestacy and gives you greater control over the destiny of your property.

Although it is unlikely, it is also possible for a residuary beneficiary to die at the same time as you or very shortly after you, usually as a result of an accident affecting you both, for example, a road accident. Your residue may pass to the residuary beneficiary and then almost immediately pass on, either under the beneficiary's Will or, if none, under the rules of intestacy, and again result in a distribution you may not have wanted. The inclusion of a survivorship clause prevents this process and allows you to decide who will inherit your property. The survivorship period can be up to six months but it is common to choose 28 days.

The survivorship clause by its nature also covers the event of the residuary beneficiary predeceasing you. The Lawpack Scotland Will Forms all contain survivorship clauses except in the case of gifts to your children.

If you give your residue initially to more than one person in shares, you need to make clear whether if one of them dies that person's share goes:

- to another person as replacement beneficiary, or
- to the survivors of the people you named initially.

In Scotland Will Form 1 the Residuary Gift reads:

> 'I GIVE the residue of my estate to _____
> but if he/she or (if I have indicated more than one person) any of them fails to survive me by 28 days or if this gift or any part of it fails for any other reason, then I GIVE the residue of my estate or the part of it affected to _____.'

So if you name another person as replacement beneficiary and any of the persons named initially dies, his or her share will pass to the replacement beneficiary. However, if you have initially named more than one person, it is probably unlikely that all of them will fail to survive you. If you want the share of any person who dies to go to the others, you should write at the end of the Residuary Gift 'the other residuary beneficiary' if you initially named only two, or 'the other residuary beneficiaries in proportion to their shares' if you initially named more than two.

> **Example:** 'I GIVE the residue of my estate to <u>David Peter Ross, Susanna Hill and Nigel Jones in equal shares</u> but if he/she or (if I have indicated more than one person) any of them fails to survive me by 28 days or if this gift or any part of it fails for any other reason, then I GIVE the residue of my estate or the part of it affected to <u>the other residuary beneficiaries in proportion to their shares.</u>'

In Scotland Will Form 2, if you name two or more adults to take initially and one dies, his or her share might be treated as passing to his or her children and therefore you should make it clear.

If this is not what you want or any of the above is not clear, you should consult a solicitor.

Disposal of property during your lifetime

People often believe that once they leave property under their Will they lose the right to sell or otherwise dispose of the property during their lifetime. This is not so. You retain the right to do whatever you choose with your property notwithstanding its mention in your Will.

> **Example:** 'I give my house, 12 Arthur's Seat, Edinburgh to my friend Peter Harrison.'

The above example means that your friend Peter only inherits 12 Arthur's Seat if you own it at the time of your death. If you sold it and bought another house, your friend would not receive the new house in its place. You may wish to cover this eventuality by saying: 'I bequeath whatever house may be my principal or ordinary residence at the time of my death to my friend Peter Harrison.'

Obviously, if your Will includes many legacies that are no longer possible to give because you no longer possess the items, it is time to prepare a new Will to dispose of the assets you do have.

Property that does not pass under your Will

Is your home jointly owned with another person? If so, is the property held under a survivorship destination or jointly owned in shares? If you are uncertain how your property is held, you should consult a solicitor. A bank account is also sometimes held in joint names. In principle, any property can be so held.

If the property is held under a survivorship destination (which means you both own the whole property), then upon your death your interest in the property automatically goes to your surviving co-owner. If your property is jointly owned (which means you each own a specified share in the property, say half and half or one third and two thirds), then you can bequeath your share in the property to whomever you wish.

> **Example of a survivorship destination in the title deeds to a property:**
> 'I dispone to and in favour of the said David Ross and Moira Ross equally between them and to the survivor of them and to the executors and assignees of the survivor whomsoever…'

> **Example of joint ownership in the title deeds to a property:**
> 'I dispone to and in favour of the said David Ross and Moira Ross and to their respective executors and assignees whomsoever…'

If you wish to do so, you can change a property held under a survivorship destination into a property held in joint ownership, but to do so you should consult a solicitor.

An individual holding property under a survivorship destination is liable to pay any tax that may be due on inheriting your share of the property, unless you specify otherwise. This does not apply to spouses or civil partners. If you do not wish the survivor to pay this tax personally, you must include the following statement in your Will:

> 'I wish the burden of any tax due on my interest in property held under a survivorship destination to fall on my residuary estate.'

Generally, life insurance policies that are expressed to be for the benefit of your spouse or civil partner and/or children do not pass under your Will and therefore do not form part of your estate. The premiums paid on such a policy are probably not taxable if paid out of normal disposable income. The policy can be written in such a way that the proceeds are not taxable when you die. A life insurance policy is a good way to provide your family with the funds to meet any tax payable upon your death. Consult an authorised Independent Financial Adviser for more details.

Your pension rights may pass outside your Will in the same way. Your employer should have more details. In many cases, you will be able to name the person who is to benefit from your pension rights, but only in a separate document, not in your Will.

Property which is situated abroad may not pass under your Will. You should consult a solicitor if you own or have an interest in property abroad.

Tax considerations in estate planning

The main tax charged upon estates is Inheritance Tax (IHT). This is a tax on all the assets held by you on your death (including joint property) as well as upon gifts made by you within seven years before your death. If those assets and gifts do not exceed the current sum of £325,000 (known as the 'nil rate band'), your estate will not pay any tax. After that sum, tax is charged at 40 per cent.

It is possible to word the provisions of a Will in a manner that will reduce the tax burden on your estate. Set out below is a simplified explanation of the tax issues facing your estate and some of the factors you should consider when drafting your Will. The explanation is for guidance only and cannot replace more detailed advice from an accountant or a solicitor. If the value of your estate substantially exceeds the nil rate band on which Inheritance Tax is not charged, you really should ask an accountant or a solicitor to advise you about any possible ways of reducing the burden of tax on your estate.

There are some exemptions from IHT. First, there is no charge on property that goes to your spouse (or registered civil partner) or to charity. Second, certain property such as business property (not including investment properties) and agricultural property are either exempt or charged at lower rates. In order to maximise those exemptions you should consider making specific gifts of business or agricultural property rather than including such property as part of the residue and ensuring that, so far as possible, those are gifts to persons other than your spouse or a charity (as such gifts are exempt anyway).

Prior to the pre-budget report on 9 October 2007 most other Will planning involved ensuring that two spouses (or civil partners) maximised the use of their nil rate bands. Following the pre-budget report, where a person leaves all their estate to their spouse the survivor will have twice the available nil rate band on their death. That means that such planning is unnecessary and indeed it is now better to leave property to a spouse than to maximise the nil rate band using vehicles such as trusts.

There are also steps you can take in your lifetime that can minimise the amount of tax you pay:

- Gifts made more than seven years before you die are not subject to IHT. Consider whether there is property that you can give away now.
- Gifts totalling up to £3,000 per annum, payable to any person, (however long the donor lives) are exempt whenever made.
- Gifts made from 'normal expenditure out of income', in other words gifts that can be said to be normal for the individual and are made solely from income are exempt whenever made.
- Gifts by parents to the parties to a marriage or civil partnership up to £5,000 are exempt.
- Gifts by a grandparent or remoter ancestor of either party up to £2,500 or gifts by any other person in consideration of marriage or civil partnership up to £1,000 are exempt gifts.
- Gifts paid to children or other family members in order to maintain them (where they are unable to do so themselves) or to pay for their education or training whilst in full-time education (an example would be the payment of a child's university fees) are exempt.

In your lifetime, you should not make any gift of a large asset (such as your home) without seeking advice. Such a lifetime gift needs care because it could cause other taxes to become payable and might not be effective for saving IHT.

Witnesses to your Will

To ensure the validity of your Will, it is important to have it properly witnessed. You need one witness who should be over 16, and his or her full name, address and occupation should be clearly stated. A blind person cannot witness a Will.

It is important that someone who is named as an executor or who benefits (or potentially benefits) under the Will should not act as a witness.

Signing your Will

You must sign your Will at the bottom of each page in the presence of one witness, who must then sign in your presence as a witness to your signature. Neither you nor the witnesses should leave the room until your Will is signed and witnessed. The witness is simply witnessing your signature and need know nothing of the contents of your Will.

Use your usual signature, write in ink and date your Will, writing out the date in full rather than in figures. Be sure that the witness completes his or her name, address and occupation in the space provided in the Scotland Will Forms.

How to revise your Will

Never attempt to revise or change your Will by altering it. The way to revise an existing Will is to prepare a new Will, or in the case of small alterations, to prepare a codicil to your Will. A new Will should contain a clause revoking all previous Wills. The Scotland Will Forms in this Kit all contain a revocation clause. For safety, however, you should also physically destroy any former Will so that it cannot be mistaken for your most recent Will. Make sure you destroy all copies of your former Will as well. If you have made a separate Will dealing with property abroad or, indeed, if you own or have an interest in property abroad, you should consult a solicitor.

Remember, you should not add words or provisions, nor should you change, delete, cross out or erase any part of your Will once it has been prepared.

Safekeeping of your Will

After completion, your Will should be kept in a safe place either at home or lodged with a bank or solicitor. Alternatively, you can use Lawpack's Will Storage Service, details of which can be found on page 63.

Make sure that you keep with your private papers a note of where your Will is held. It is sensible to keep a photocopy of your Will in case the original is accidentally lost or destroyed, but it should be clear that it is only a copy.

What happens when someone dies?

When someone dies the Will should be reviewed as soon as possible, as it may contain directions with regard to the funeral arrangements (or organ donation).

After the funeral has taken place, a meeting with a solicitor should be arranged to discuss the administration of the deceased's estate. To enable the solicitor to gather all the information required, give the solicitor every document belonging to the deceased that concerns money or property, the Will, any other record-keeping forms, share certificates, bank account details, building society passbooks, life insurance policies, mortgage papers, pension scheme details and any other relevant document. The solicitor will then assist the executors to obtain Confirmation.

Where the value of the deceased's estate does not exceed £30,000 the Sheriff Clerk at the appropriate Sheriff Court will assist the executors to obtain Confirmation and solicitors' fees can thereby be avoided. Confirmation is the executors' authority to uplift (secure the release of) funds held in the deceased's name and to distribute the estate in accordance with the deceased's wishes. To obtain Confirmation, the deceased's assets at the date of death are listed in a document known as the Inventory (or C1 Account). The Inventory (along with C5 Account, unless it has been necessary to complete Form IHT400 which would have to be submitted to the Capital Taxes Office) and the Will (and any subsequent codicils) are signed by one of the executors and are then lodged in the Sheriff Court responsible for the area in which the deceased died. Confirmation is granted in the name(s) of the deceased's executors, who can then proceed with the administration of the estate. At the end of the administration, it is the executors' responsibility to prepare accounts showing how the estate has been distributed.

Using the Scotland Will Forms

You should now be ready to draft your Will.

Select the worksheet corresponding to the Will Form that is appropriate to your circumstances and requirements. This depends upon whom you wish to receive the residue of your estate.

Scotland Will Form 1	should be used if you want to give the residue of your estate to an adult, and provide for another adult to take instead if the first fails to survive you by 28 days. This Form may also be used to give your residue to a charity.
Scotland Will Form 2	should be used if you want to give the residue of your estate to an adult, and provide for your children to take instead in equal shares if the adult fails to survive you by 28 days.
Scotland Will Form 3	should be used if you want to give the residue of your estate to your children in equal shares in any event.

Using the worksheets, prepare a rough copy first. Make any necessary corrections. When you are satisfied with your final version complete the appropriate Will Form. Type it or write in ink. If you prefer, you can download Will Forms 1, 2 and 3 and the template documents included in this Kit. For further details please see enclosed flyer. Once completed, follow precisely the correct procedure as to signature, dating and witnessing to validate your Last Will & Testament.

Glossary

adult – under Scottish law, a person aged 16 or over.

beneficiary – a person who receives all or part of an estate under a Will. A beneficiary may also be a person who receives payment from a life insurance policy or a trust.

civil partnership – a partnership registered under the Civil Partnership Act 2004.

civil partners – persons who are registered as partners under the Civil Partnership Act 2004.

codicil – a document that amends and often adds to a Will.

Confirmation – authority granted by the court to the executors to administer the deceased's estate.

dispone – to transfer or give.

encumbrance – usually a mortgage or charge upon property securing the payment of a debt or other liability.

estate – all the property belonging to a person at death.

Executor Dative – a person appointed by the court to manage the estate of a deceased person when there is no executor nominate.

Executor Nominate – a person named in a Will to manage the deceased's estate.

guardian – a person with parental responsibility for a minor child.

Inheritance Tax – a tax imposed on a person's estate upon death and in some cases on gifts during the person's lifetime.

intestate – dying without leaving a valid Will.

joint property – property owned jointly with another person or persons.

legal rights – the claims which the surviving spouse and/or issue have to share in the deceased's estate, whether or not the deceased died intestate.

obtaining Confirmation – the process of proving the validity of a Will, and the executor's authority to manage the estate, by application to the local Sheriff Court.

pecuniary legacy – a gift of money in a Will.

per stirpes – division between a number of beneficiaries according to branches of the family, as opposed to equally among all the beneficiaries.

replacement beneficiary – a person designated as a beneficiary if someone else predeceases the testator or fails to survive the testator for a specified period or to reach a specified age.

residuary beneficiary – a beneficiary who receives the residue of an estate or part of it.

residuary gift – a gift of residue made in a Will.

residue – the remainder of an estate after the deduction of tax, debts, specific bequests, legacies, any legal rights payments and the expenses of administration.

specific gift – a gift of a particular item of property in a Will.

substitutional beneficiary – a person designated as a beneficiary if someone else predeceases the testator or fails to survive the testator for a specified period or to reach a specified age.

testator – a person who makes a Will.

trust – an arrangement under which a person or persons (the trustee or trustees) hold and manage property for the benefit of another person or persons (the trust beneficiary or beneficiaries).

Will – a legal document which sets out the wishes of the testator for the distribution of his or her estate and certain other matters after his or her death.

witness – a person who signs a Will to signify that he saw the testator sign it.

Example of completed Scotland Will Form 1

Last Will & Testament

SCOTLAND WILL FORM 1 – SIMPLE GIFT OF THE RESIDUE

PRINT FULL NAME AND ADDRESS
THIS Last Will & Testament is made by me RICHARD BERNARD ROSS of 28 STAPLEFORTH ROAD, EDINBURGH EH22 4LJ

I REVOKE all previous wills and codicils.

EXECUTORS' FULL NAMES AND ADDRESSES
I APPOINT as executors and trustees of my will
name DAVID PETER ROSS and name ANTHONY WILLIAMS
of 5 MAPLE TERRACE of 17 ST GEORGE'S CRESCENT
EDINBURGH EH10 2PZ ABERDEEN AB7 9XY

REPLACEMENT EXECUTOR'S NAME AND ADDRESS
and should one or more of them fail to or be unable to act I APPOINT to fill any vacancy
name GILLIAN ROSS
of 5 MAPLE TERRACE, EDINBURGH EH10 2PZ

DEBTS AND FUNERAL EXPENSES
I direct my executors to settle my debts and funeral expenses and the expenses of administering my estate;

SPECIFIC GIFTS AND PECUNIARY LEGACIES
I GIVE MY COTTAGE (OR MY WHOLE INTEREST THEREIN) AT ST ANDREWS, FIFE TO MY BROTHER DAVID PETER ROSS, RESIDING AT 122 ALBION DRIVE, EDINBURGH, FREE FROM ANY MORTGAGE (ANY MORTGAGE BEING REPAID OUT OF THE RESIDUE OF MY ESTATE). THREE THOUSAND POUNDS TO MY FRIEND, ANTHONY WILLIAMS, RESIDING AT 3 FOREST AVENUE, ST ANDREWS.

(Testator's Signature)

Example of completed Scotland Will Form 1 (continued)

RESIDUARY GIFT — I GIVE the residue of my estate to JAMES ALEXANDER ROSS RESIDING AT 52 HILL DRIVE, EDINBURGH, SUSANNA HILL RESIDING AT 22 THE CRESCENT, DUNDEE AND NIGEL JONES RESIDING AT 14 NEW ROAD, GLASGOW IN EQUAL SHARES

but if he/she or (if I have indicated more than one person) any of them fails to survive me by 28 days or if this gift or any part of it fails for any other reason, then I GIVE the residue of my estate or the part of it affected to THE OTHER RESIDUARY BENEFICIARIES IN PROPORTION TO THEIR SHARES

EXECUTORS' POWERS — And my executors shall have all the powers of gratuitous trustees;

With reference to these presents I HEREBY DECLARE as follows, videlicet:-

That all pecuniary legacies shall be payable without interest and within six months of the date of my death;

That all specific bequests shall be subject to the beneficiary paying the delivery costs;

FUNERAL WISHES — I WISH my body to be ✔ buried ☐ cremated ☐ other instructions AT ST ANDREWS OLD CHURCH, EDINBURGH

And in the event of my death, (not survived by my wife/husband),

GUARDIAN'S FULL NAME AND ADDRESS — I NOMINATE and APPOINT NONE of _____

to be guardian to such of my children as are under the age of full legal capacity at my death;

DATE — IN WITNESS WHEREOF these presents written on this and the preceding page are subscribed by me at address 28 STAPLEFORTH RD EDINBURGH EH10 2PZ

on the 10TH day of OCTOBER TWO THOUSAND AND ELEVEN before this witness:-

TESTATOR'S SIGNATURE — SIGNED _(signature)_

WITNESS'S SIGNATURE — SIGNED _(signature)_

WITNESS'S FULL NAME AND ADDRESS — name RUTH ELIZABETH GRANT
of 90 WEIR MANSIONS
EDINBURGH EH12 2BS
occupation HOUSEWIFE

Last Will & Testament

SCOTLAND WILL FORM 1 – SIMPLE GIFT OF THE RESIDUE

PRINT FULL NAME AND ADDRESS

THIS Last Will & Testament is made by me _____

of _____

I REVOKE all previous wills and codicils.

EXECUTORS' FULL NAMES AND ADDRESSES

I APPOINT as executors and trustees of my will

name _____ and name _____

of _____ of _____

_____ _____

REPLACEMENT EXECUTOR'S NAME AND ADDRESS

and should one or more of them fail to or be unable to act I APPOINT to fill any vacancy

name _____

of _____

DEBTS AND FUNERAL EXPENSES

I direct my executors to settle my debts and funeral expenses and the expenses of administering my estate;

SPECIFIC GIFTS AND PECUNIARY LEGACIES

I GIVE _____

_____

_____

_____

_____

_____

_____

_____

_____

_____

_____

_____

_____

_____

_____
(Testator's Signature)

RESIDUARY GIFT   I GIVE the residue of my estate to _____

_____

_____

but if he/she or (if I have indicated more than one person) any of them fails to survive me by 28 days or if this gift or any part of it fails for any other reason, then I GIVE the residue of my estate or the part of it affected to

_____

EXECUTORS' POWERS   And my executors shall have all the powers of gratuitous trustees;

With reference to these presents I HEREBY DECLARE as follows, videlicet:-

That all pecuniary legacies shall be payable without interest and within six months of the date of my death;

That all specific bequests shall be subject to the beneficiary paying the delivery costs;

FUNERAL WISHES   I WISH my body to be ☐ buried ☐ cremated ☐ other instructions _____

_____

And in the event of my death, (not survived by my wife/husband),

GUARDIAN'S FULL NAME AND ADDRESS   I NOMINATE and APPOINT _____

of _____

to be guardian to such of my children as are under the age of full legal capacity at my death;

DATE   IN WITNESS WHEREOF these presents written on this and the preceding page are subscribed by me at

address _____

_____

on the _____ day of _____

_____ before this witness:-

TESTATOR'S SIGNATURE   SIGNED_____

WITNESS'S SIGNATURE   SIGNED_____

WITNESS'S FULL NAME AND ADDRESS   name _____

of _____

_____

occupation _____

Example of completed Scotland Will Form 2

Last Will & Testament

SCOTLAND WILL FORM 2 - RESIDUE TO AN ADULT BUT IF HE/SHE DIES TO CHILDREN

PRINT FULL NAME AND ADDRESS
THIS Last Will & Testament is made by me GILLIAN ROSS
of 5 MAPLE TERRACE, EDINBURGH EH10 2PZ

I REVOKE all previous wills and codicils.

EXECUTORS' FULL NAMES AND ADDRESSES
I APPOINT as executors and trustees of my will
name DAVID PETER ROSS and name THERESA MUNDY
of 5 MAPLE TERRACE of 9 KING'S WALK
EDINBURGH EH10 2PZ GLASGOW G9 4BL

REPLACEMENT EXECUTOR'S NAME AND ADDRESS
and should one or more of them fail to or be unable to act I APPOINT to fill any vacancy
name THOMAS JAMES WAITE
of 36 AMBER ROAD, EDINBURGH EH3 5HM

DEBTS AND FUNERAL EXPENSES
I direct my executors and trustees to settle my debts and funeral expenses and the expenses of administering my estate;

SPECIFIC GIFTS AND PECUNIARY LEGACIES
I GIVE ALL OF MY JEWELLERY TO MY DAUGHTER MARY JANE ROSS RESIDING AT 5 MAPLE TERRACE, EDINBURGH EH10 2PZ. ONE THOUSAND POUNDS TO EACH OF MY SONS, JAMES TARQUIN ROSS AND ALEXANDER ROSS, BOTH RESIDING AT 5 MAPLE TERRACE, EDINBURGH EH10 2PZ. MY MOTOR CAR, REGISTRATION NUMBER W288 YVV, TO MY FRIEND, PETER MACLEOD, RESIDING AT 24 WEST STREET, PERTH.

RESIDUARY GIFT
I GIVE the residue of my estate to MY HUSBAND DAVID PETER ROSS

(insert age at which you want your children to inherit capital)
but if he/she or (if I have indicated more than one person) any of them fails to survive me by 28 days or if this gift or any part of it fails for any other reason, then I direct my trustees to pay, convey and make over the said residue so far as not disposed of equally between or among or wholly to such of my children as survive the coming into operation of this Clause, and have then attained or thereafter attain the age of 21 years complete, along with the issue who do so survive and attain the said age of any of my children who may fail to so survive or do so survive but fail to attain the said age, such issue taking equally between or among them "per stirpes" if more than one the share of residue, original and accrescing, such as the parent would have taken on survivance;

Gillian Ross
(Testator's Signature)

Example of completed Scotland Will Form 2 (continued)

TRUSTEES' POWERS
(insert age at which you want your children to inherit capital)

DECLARING that during the minority of any beneficiary hereunder (which for this purpose shall be while such beneficiary is under the age of _21_ years complete) who is prospectively entitled to a share of the capital of the said residue in terms of this Clause, my trustees shall apply so much, if any, of the income of the share of capital to which he or she is for the time being prospectively entitled as they in their absolute discretion may from time to time consider to be necessary for his or her maintenance, education or benefit and my trustees shall accumulate so much of the said income as is not applied for the foregoing purposes and add the same to the capital of such share; and

(insert age at which you want your children to become entitled to receive the income)

That on the attainment of the age of _18_ years complete of any beneficiary hereunder who is prospectively entitled to a share of the capital of the said residue, my trustees shall, until he or she becomes entitled to receive the said capital, pay to him or her the whole income of the said capital to which he or she is for the time being prospectively entitled and the whole income of any accumulations thereon; and

With reference to these presents I Hereby Declare as follows, videlicet:-

That all pecuniary legacies shall be payable without interest and within six months of the date of my death;

That all specific bequests shall be subject to the beneficiary paying the delivery costs;

That no beneficiary shall take a vested interest in any part of the said residue until the term or terms of payment thereof except that all payments or advances which may be made by my trustees by virtue of the powers herein conferred on them shall vest in the beneficiary receiving the same at the date of payment or advance;

That my trustees shall have power in their absolute discretion to advance to any residuary beneficiary hereunder, any part or even the whole of his or her prospective share of the said residue for any purpose which my trustees shall deem to be for his or her permanent advantage or benefit and on such terms and conditions, as my trustees in their uncontrolled discretion think fit;

That my trustees shall have power to pay and make over in whole or in part any funds due or advanced to or on account of any beneficiary under the age of full legal capacity to his or her legal guardian, the receipt of such guardian constituting a sufficient discharge.

That there shall be no apportionment of income between capital and revenue on any occasion, all income being deemed to have accrued at the date upon which it is payable;

And I PROVIDE and DECLARE that my trustees shall have all the powers and immunities of gratuitous trustees and shall not be restricted to investments authorised by the Trustee Investments Act 1961;

FUNERAL WISHES
I WISH my body to be ☐ buried ☑ cremated ☐ other instructions _____

And in the event of my death, (not survived by my wife/husband),

GUARDIAN'S FULL NAME AND ADDRESS
I NOMINATE AND APPOINT _THERESA MUNDY_
of _9 KING'S WALK, GLASGOW G9 4BL_

to be the guardian to such of my children as are under the age of full legal capacity at my death;

DATE
IN WITNESS WHEREOF these presents written on this and the preceding page are subscribed by me at
address _5 MAPLE TERRACE, EDINBURGH EH10 2PZ_
on the _10TH_ day of _OCTOBER_
TWO THOUSAND AND ELEVEN before this witness:-

TESTATOR'S SIGNATURE
SIGNED _Gillian Ross_

WITNESS'S SIGNATURE
SIGNED _Ruth Grant_

WITNESS'S FULL NAME AND ADDRESS
name _RUTH ELIZABETH GRANT_
of _90 WEIR MANSIONS_
EDINBURGH EH12 2BS
occupation _HOUSEWIFE_

Last Will & Testament

SCOTLAND WILL FORM 2 - RESIDUE TO AN ADULT BUT IF HE/SHE DIES TO CHILDREN

PRINT FULL NAME AND ADDRESS

THIS Last Will & Testament is made by me _____

of _____

I REVOKE all previous wills and codicils.

EXECUTORS' FULL NAMES AND ADDRESSES

I APPOINT as executors and trustees of my will

name _____ and name _____

of _____ of _____

_____ _____

REPLACEMENT EXECUTOR'S NAME AND ADDRESS

and should one or more of them fail to or be unable to act I APPOINT to fill any vacancy

name _____

of _____

DEBTS AND FUNERAL EXPENSES

I direct my executors and trustees to settle my debts and funeral expenses and the expenses of administering my estate;

SPECIFIC GIFTS AND PECUNIARY LEGACIES

I GIVE _____

_____

_____

_____

_____

_____

_____

_____

_____

_____

RESIDUARY GIFT

I GIVE the residue of my estate to _____

_____

(insert age at which you want your children to inherit capital)

but if he/she or (if I have indicated more than one person) any of them fails to survive me by 28 days or if this gift or any part of it fails for any other reason, then I direct my trustees to pay, convey and make over the said residue so far as not disposed of equally between or among or wholly to such of my children as survive the coming into operation of this Clause, and have then attained or thereafter attain the age of _____ years complete, along with the issue who do so survive and attain the said age of any of my children who may fail to so survive or do so survive but fail to attain the said age, such issue taking equally between or among them "per stirpes" if more than one the share of residue, original and accrescing, such as the parent would have taken on survivance;

_____

(Testator's Signature)

TRUSTEES' POWERS
(insert age at which you want your children to inherit capital)

DECLARING that during the minority of any beneficiary hereunder (which for this purpose shall be while such beneficiary is under the age of _____ years complete) who is prospectively entitled to a share of the capital of the said residue in terms of this Clause, my trustees shall apply so much, if any, of the income of the share of capital to which he or she is for the time being prospectively entitled as they in their absolute discretion may from time to time consider to be necessary for his or her maintenance, education or benefit and my trustees shall accumulate so much of the said income as is not applied for the foregoing purposes and add the same to the capital of such share; and

(insert age at which you want your children to become entitled to receive the income)

That on the attainment of the age of _____ years complete of any beneficiary hereunder who is prospectively entitled to a share of the capital of the said residue, my trustees shall, until he or she becomes entitled to receive the said capital, pay to him or her the whole income of the said capital to which he or she is for the time being prospectively entitled and the whole income of any accumulations thereon; and

With reference to these presents I Hereby Declare as follows, videlicet:

That all pecuniary legacies shall be payable without interest and within six months of the date of my death;

That all specific bequests shall be subject to the beneficiary paying the delivery costs;

That no beneficiary shall take a vested interest in any part of the said residue until the term or terms of payment thereof except that all payments or advances which may be made by my trustees by virtue of the powers herein conferred on them shall vest in the beneficiary receiving the same at the date of payment or advance;

That my trustees shall have power in their absolute discretion to advance to any residuary beneficiary hereunder, any part or even the whole of his or her prospective share of the said residue for any purpose which my trustees shall deem to be for his or her permanent advantage or benefit and on such terms and conditions, as my trustees in their uncontrolled discretion think fit;

That my trustees shall have power to pay and make over in whole or in part any funds due or advanced to or on account of any beneficiary under the age of full legal capacity to his or her legal guardian, the receipt of such guardian constituting a sufficient discharge.

That there shall be no apportionment of income between capital and revenue on any occasion, all income being deemed to have accrued at the date upon which it is payable;

And I PROVIDE and DECLARE that my trustees shall have all the powers and immunities of gratuitous trustees and shall not be restricted to investments authorised by the Trustee Investments Act 1961;

FUNERAL WISHES

I WISH my body to be ☐ buried ☐ cremated ☐ other instructions _____
_____

And in the event of my death, (not survived by my wife/husband),

GUARDIAN'S FULL NAME AND ADDRESS

I NOMINATE AND APPOINT _____

of _____

to be the guardian to such of my children as are under the age of full legal capacity at my death;

DATE

IN WITNESS WHEREOF these presents written on this and the preceding page are subscribed by me at

address _____

on the _____ day of _____

_____ before this witness:

TESTATOR'S SIGNATURE

SIGNED _____

WITNESS'S SIGNATURE

SIGNED _____

WITNESS'S FULL NAME AND ADDRESS

name _____

of _____

_____

occupation _____

Example of completed Scotland Will Form 3

Last Will & Testament

SCOTLAND WILL FORM 3 - RESIDUE DIRECT TO CHILDREN

PRINT FULL NAME AND ADDRESS

THIS Last Will & Testament is made by me GILLIAN ROSS

of 5 MAPLE TERRACE, EDINBURGH EH10 2PZ

I REVOKE all previous wills and codicils.

EXECUTORS' FULL NAMES AND ADDRESSES

I APPOINT as executors and trustees of my will

name DAVID PETER ROSS and name THERESA MUNDY

of 5 MAPLE TERRACE of 9 KING'S WALK

EDINBURGH EH10 2PZ GLASGOW G9 4BL

REPLACEMENT EXECUTOR'S NAME AND ADDRESS

and should one or more of them fail to or be unable to act I APPOINT to fill any vacancy

name THOMAS JAMES WAITE

of 36 AMBER ROAD, EDINBURGH EH3 5MM

DEBTS AND FUNERAL EXPENSES

I direct my executors and trustees to settle my debts and funeral expenses and the expenses of administering my estate;

SPECIFIC GIFTS AND PECUNIARY LEGACIES

I GIVE ALL MY JEWELLERY TO MY DAUGHTER MARY JANE ROSS RESIDING AT 5 MAPLE TERRACE, EDINBURGH EH10 2PZ. FIVE THOUSAND POUNDS TO EACH OF MY SONS, JAMES TARQUIN ROSS AND ALEXANDER GUY ROSS, BOTH RESIDING AT 5 MAPLE TERRACE, EDINBURGH EH10 2PZ. MY HOUSE (OR MY WHOLE INTEREST THEREIN) AT 5 MAPLE TERRACE, EDINBURGH EH10 2PZ TO MY HUSBAND, DAVID PETER ROSS, RESIDING AT 5 MAPLE TERRACE EDINBURGH EH10 2PZ SUBJECT TO ANY EXISTING MORTGAGE ON IT.

RESIDUARY GIFT

(insert age at which you want your children to inherit capital)

I direct my trustees to pay, convey and make over the residue of my estate equally between or among or wholly to such of my children as survive the coming into operation of this Clause, and have then attained or thereafter attain the age of 18 years complete, along with the issue who do so survive and attain the said age of any of my children who may fail to so survive or do so survive but fail to attain the said age, such issue taking equally between or among them "per stirpes" if more than one the share of residue, original and accrescing, such as the parent would have taken on survivance;

Gillian Ross

(Testator's Signature)

Example of completed Scotland Will Form 3 (continued)

TRUSTEES' POWERS
(insert age at which you want your children to inherit capital)

DECLARING that during the minority of any beneficiary hereunder (which for this purpose shall be while such beneficiary is under the age of 21 years complete) who is prospectively entitled to a share of the capital of the said residue in terms of this Clause, my trustees shall apply so much, if any, of the income of the share of capital to which he or she is for the time being prospectively entitled as they in their absolute discretion may from time to time consider to be necessary for his or her maintenance, education or benefit and my trustees shall accumulate so much of the said income as is not applied for the foregoing purposes and add the same to the capital of such share; and

(insert age at which you want your children to become entitled to receive the income)

That on the attainment of the age of 18 years complete of any beneficiary hereunder who is prospectively entitled to a share of the capital of the said residue, my trustees shall, until he or she becomes entitled to receive the said capital, pay to him or her the whole income of the said capital to which he or she is for the time being prospectively entitled and the whole income of any accumulations thereon; and

With reference to these presents I Hereby Declare as follows, videlicet:-

That all pecuniary legacies shall be payable without interest and within six months of the date of my death;

That all specific bequests shall be subject to the beneficiary paying the delivery costs;

That no beneficiary shall take a vested interest in any part of the said residue until the term or terms of payment thereof except that all payments or advances which may be made by my trustees by virtue of the powers herein conferred on them shall vest in the beneficiary receiving the same at the date of payment or advance;

That my trustees shall have power in their absolute discretion to advance to any residuary beneficiary hereunder, any part or even the whole of his or her prospective share of the said residue for any purpose which my trustees shall deem to be for his or her permanent advantage or benefit and on such terms and conditions, as my trustees in their uncontrolled discretion think fit;

That my trustees shall have power to pay and make over in whole or in part any funds due or advanced to or on account of any beneficiary under the age of full legal capacity to his or her legal guardian, the receipt of such guardian constituting a sufficient discharge.

That there shall be no apportionment of income between capital and revenue on any occasion, all income being deemed to have accrued at the date upon which it is payable;

And I PROVIDE and DECLARE that my trustees shall have all the powers and immunities of gratuitous trustees and shall not be restricted to investments authorised by the Trustee Investments Act 1961;

FUNERAL WISHES   I WISH my body to be ☐ buried ☑ cremated ☐ other instructions _____

And in the event of my death, (not survived by my wife/husband),

GUARDIAN'S FULL NAME AND ADDRESS

I NOMINATE AND APPOINT THERESA HUNDY
of 9 KING'S WALK, GLASGOW G9 4BL

to be guardian to such of my children as are under the age of full legal capacity at my death;

DATE   IN WITNESS WHEREOF these presents written on this and the preceding page are subscribed by me at

address 5 MAPLE TERRACE, EDINBURGH EH10 2PZ

on the 10TH day of OCTOBER

TWO THOUSAND AND ELEVEN _____ before this witness:-

TESTATOR'S SIGNATURE   SIGNED _Gillian Ross_

WITNESS'S SIGNATURE   SIGNED _Ruth Grant_

WITNESS'S FULL NAME AND ADDRESS

name RUTH ELIZABETH GRANT
of 90 WEIR MANSIONS
EDINBURGH EH12 2BS
occupation HOUSEWIFE

Last Will & Testament

SCOTLAND WILL FORM 3 - RESIDUE DIRECT TO CHILDREN

PRINT FULL NAME AND ADDRESS

THIS Last Will & Testament is made by me _____

of _____

I REVOKE all previous wills and codicils.

EXECUTORS' FULL NAMES AND ADDRESSES

I APPOINT as executors and trustees of my will

name _____ and name _____

of _____ of _____

_____ _____

REPLACEMENT EXECUTOR'S NAME AND ADDRESS

and should one or more of them fail to or be unable to act I APPOINT to fill any vacancy

name _____

of _____

DEBTS AND FUNERAL EXPENSES

I direct my executors and trustees to settle my debts and funeral expenses and the expenses of administering my estate;

SPECIFIC GIFTS AND PECUNIARY LEGACIES

I GIVE _____

_____

_____

_____

_____

_____

_____

_____

_____

_____

_____

RESIDUARY GIFT

(insert age at which you want your children to inherit capital)

I direct my trustees to pay, convey and make over the residue of my estate equally between or among or wholly to such of my children as survive the coming into operation of this Clause, and have then attained or thereafter attain the age of _____ years complete, along with the issue who do so survive and attain the said age of any of my children who may fail to so survive or do so survive but fail to attain the said age, such issue taking equally between or among them "per stirpes" if more than one the share of residue, original and accrescing, such as the parent would have taken on survivance;

_____

(Testator's Signature)

TRUSTEES' POWERS (insert age at which you want your children to inherit capital)

DECLARING that during the minority of any beneficiary hereunder (which for this purpose shall be while such beneficiary is under the age of _____ years complete) who is prospectively entitled to a share of the capital of the said residue in terms of this Clause, my trustees shall apply so much, if any, of the income of the share of capital to which he or she is for the time being prospectively entitled as they in their absolute discretion may from time to time consider to be necessary for his or her maintenance, education or benefit and my trustees shall accumulate so much of the said income as is not applied for the foregoing purposes and add the same to the capital of such share; and

(insert age at which you want your children to become entitled to receive the income)

That on the attainment of the age of _____ years complete of any beneficiary hereunder who is prospectively entitled to a share of the capital of the said residue, my trustees shall, until he or she becomes entitled to receive the said capital, pay to him or her the whole income of the said capital to which he or she is for the time being prospectively entitled and the whole income of any accumulations thereon; and

With reference to these presents I Hereby Declare as follows, videlicet:

That all pecuniary legacies shall be payable without interest and within six months of the date of my death;

That all specific bequests shall be subject to the beneficiary paying the delivery costs;

That no beneficiary shall take a vested interest in any part of the said residue until the term or terms of payment thereof except that all payments or advances which may be made by my trustees by virtue of the powers herein conferred on them shall vest in the beneficiary receiving the same at the date of payment or advance;

That my trustees shall have power in their absolute discretion to advance to any residuary beneficiary hereunder, any part or even the whole of his or her prospective share of the said residue for any purpose which my trustees shall deem to be for his or her permanent advantage or benefit and on such terms and conditions, as my trustees in their uncontrolled discretion think fit;

That my trustees shall have power to pay and make over in whole or in part any funds due or advanced to or on account of any beneficiary under the age of full legal capacity to his or her legal guardian, the receipt of such guardian constituting a sufficient discharge.

That there shall be no apportionment of income between capital and revenue on any occasion, all income being deemed to have accrued at the date upon which it is payable;

And I PROVIDE and DECLARE that my trustees shall have all the powers and immunities of gratuitous trustees and shall not be restricted to investments authorised by the Trustee Investments Act 1961;

FUNERAL WISHES

I WISH my body to be ☐ buried ☐ cremated ☐ other instructions _____

_____

And in the event of my death, (not survived by my wife/husband),

GUARDIAN'S FULL NAME AND ADDRESS

I NOMINATE AND APPOINT _____

of _____

to be guardian to such of my children as are under the age of full legal capacity at my death;

DATE

IN WITNESS WHEREOF these presents written on this and the preceding page are subscribed by me at

address _____

on the _____ day of _____

_____ before this witness:

TESTATOR'S SIGNATURE

SIGNED _____

WITNESS'S SIGNATURE

SIGNED _____

WITNESS'S FULL NAME AND ADDRESS

name _____

of _____

_____

occupation _____

Form of Letter to Executor

Dear _____

I am writing to confirm that I have named you as executor of my Will dated _____ 20 _____ .

- A copy of my Will is enclosed.
- My signed original Will has been lodged with _____ .
- I have named _____ as a co-executor.*
- My solicitor is _____ at _____ .*

Please confirm to me in writing that you are willing to act as my executor.

Yours sincerely

_____

* delete as necessary

Warning: do not include any other instructions to your executors in this letter.

Funeral Wishes
of

Name _____

Funeral (Burial/Cremation) _____

Undertaker _____

Place of Service _____
_____

Type of Service _____
_____

Person Officiating _____

Music Selection _____
_____

Reading Selection _____
_____
_____

Flowers _____
_____

Special Instructions _____
_____
_____
_____

IF CREMATION, INSTRUCTIONS FOR DISPOSAL OF ASHES _____

Location of Important Documents and Summary of Personal Information

Name _____

Will _____
_____

Birth Certificate _____
_____

Marriage Certificate _____
_____

Divorce Decree _____
_____

Title Deeds _____
_____

Mortgage Documents _____
_____

Life Insurance Policies _____
_____

Pension Details _____
_____

Share Certificates _____
_____

Other Investment Certificates _____
_____

Loan and H.P. Agreements _____
_____

Bank Account Details _____
_____

Building Society Passbooks _____
_____

Donor Cards _____
_____

Passport _____
_____

Important People to Notify

Executor's Name _____

Address _____
_____
_____

Executor's Name _____

Address _____
_____
_____

Guardian's Name _____

Address _____
_____
_____

Solicitor _____

Life Insurance Company _____

Building Society _____

Bank _____

Accountant _____
_____

Property Inventory of

Name _____

Item	Estimated Value	Location
_____	_____	_____
_____	_____	_____
_____	_____	_____
_____	_____	_____
_____	_____	_____
_____	_____	_____
_____	_____	_____
_____	_____	_____
_____	_____	_____
_____	_____	_____
_____	_____	_____
_____	_____	_____
_____	_____	_____
_____	_____	_____
_____	_____	_____
_____	_____	_____
_____	_____	_____
_____	_____	_____
_____	_____	_____
_____	_____	_____
_____	_____	_____
_____	_____	_____
_____	_____	_____
_____	_____	_____
_____	_____	_____
_____	_____	_____
_____	_____	_____
_____	_____	_____

Security and peace of mind for you and your family

Lawpack Will Storage

12 MONTHS' FREE WILL STORAGE WORTH £12.00

The original copy of your Will is an important document and needs to be stored securely. You may have thought of storing it at home – but what if it becomes lost or is stolen? And would it remain completely confidential? Storing your Will with a local solicitor or bank could be the answer, but this may be inconvenient and costly. And if you move out of the area, how would your executors know where to find it?

Lawpack's Will Storage Service offers you a simple and secure solution, giving complete protection to your Will with no time limit.

- Using Lawpack's Will Storage Service your Will will be stored at Lawpack's fire-proof, secure storage facility.
- Your Will is held in a sealed envelope with a unique barcode, so that it can be retrieved instantly. If you need to make changes, your Will can be despatched to you within two working days, by post.
- With your consent, we inform your executors where your Will is stored and make sure that only he or she can retrieve it after death.
- If you instruct us to do so, we can inform your chosen charities about bequests or legacies included in your Will. Charities appreciate this service.

With your first year's storage **FREE** (and subsequently £12.00 a year), we will store your Will, giving you the peace of mind of knowing that your last wishes are in safe hands.

How to apply

Apply today by telephone, email, online or by post, quoting '**Free Will Storage**'. You will then receive your comprehensive Will Storage Pack, containing full instructions, and storage envelope.

Tel: 020 7394 4040
Email: will-storage@lawpack.co.uk
Online: www.lawpack.co.uk/willstorage
Address: Lawpack Will Storage, 76-89 Alscot Road, London, SE1 3AW

© 2011 Lawpack Publishing Limited
76-89 Alscot Road, London SE1 3AW
www.lawpack.co.uk

Last Will & Testament

ENGLAND, WALES & NORTHERN IRELAND WILL FORM 1 – SIMPLE GIFT OF THE RESIDUE

PRINT NAME AND ADDRESS

THIS Last Will & Testament is made by me _____

of _____

I REVOKE all previous wills and codicils.

EXECUTORS' NAMES AND ADDRESSES

I APPOINT as executors and trustees of my will

_____ and _____

of _____ of _____

_____ _____

REPLACEMENT EXECUTOR'S NAME AND ADDRESS

and should one or more of them fail to or be unable to act I APPOINT to fill any vacancy

_____

of _____

SPECIFIC GIFTS AND LEGACIES

I GIVE _____

_____

_____

_____

_____

_____

_____

_____

_____

_____

_____

_____

_____

_____

_____

_____

_____

_____

RESIDUARY GIFT   I GIVE the rest of my estate to my executors and trustees to hold on trust to pay my debts, taxes and testamentary expenses and pay the residue to _____

_____

_____

but if he/she or (if I have indicated more than one person) any of them fails to survive me by 28 days or if this gift or any part of it fails for any other reason, then I GIVE the residue of my estate or the part of it affected to

_____

FUNERAL WISHES   I WISH my body to be   ☐ buried   ☐ cremated   ☐ other instructions _____

_____

DATE   SIGNED by the above-named testator in our presence on the

_____ day of _____ 20 _____

and then by us in the testator's presence

TESTATOR'S SIGNATURE   SIGNED _____

WITNESSES' SIGNATURES NAMES AND ADDRESSES

SIGNED _____   SIGNED _____

_____   _____

of _____   of _____

_____   _____

occupation _____   occupation _____

© 2010 Lawpack Publishing Limited
www.lawpack.co.uk

1003751

Last Will & Testament

ENGLAND, WALES & NORTHERN IRELAND WILL FORM 2 - RESIDUE TO AN ADULT BUT IF HE/SHE DIES TO CHILDREN

PRINT NAME AND ADDRESS

THIS Last Will & Testament is made by me _____

of _____

I REVOKE all previous wills and codicils.

EXECUTORS' NAMES AND ADDRESSES

I APPOINT as executors and trustees of my will

_____ and _____

of _____ of _____

REPLACEMENT EXECUTOR'S NAME AND ADDRESS

and should one or more of them fail to or be unable to act I APPOINT to fill any vacancy

_____

of _____

GUARDIAN'S NAME AND ADDRESS

I APPOINT _____

of _____

to be guardian of any of my children who are minors if my husband/wife dies before me.

SPECIFIC GIFTS AND LEGACIES

I GIVE _____

_____

_____

_____

_____

_____

_____

_____

_____

_____

_____

_____

_____

_____

RESIDUARY GIFT I GIVE the rest of my estate to my executors and trustees to hold on trust to pay my debts, taxes and testamentary expenses and pay the residue to

_____

(insert age at which you want your children to inherit capital) but if he/she or (if I have indicated more than one person) any of them fails to survive me by 28 days or if this gift or any part of it fails for any other reason, then I GIVE the residue of my estate or the part of it affected to those of my children who survive me and attain the age of _____ years if more than one in equal shares.

PROVIDED THAT if any of my children dies before me or after me but under that age, I GIVE the share that child would have taken to his or her own children who attain 18 equally. If no person shall inherit the residue of my estate or part of it under the preceding gifts, I GIVE it to

_____

TRUSTEES' POWERS My trustees shall have the power to apply for the benefit of any beneficiary as my trustees shall in their absolute discretion think fit the whole or any part of the capital to which such beneficiary is or may in the future be entitled.

FUNERAL WISHES I WISH my body to be   ☐ buried   ☐ cremated   ☐ other instructions _____

_____

DATE SIGNED by the above-named testator in our presence on the

_____ day of _____ 20 _____

and then by us in the testator's presence

TESTATOR'S SIGNATURE SIGNED _____

WITNESSES' SIGNATURES NAMES AND ADDRESSES

SIGNED _____   SIGNED _____

_____   _____

of _____   of _____

_____   _____

occupation _____   occupation _____

© 2010 Lawpack Publishing Limited
www.lawpack.co.uk

1003751

Last Will & Testament

ENGLAND, WALES & NORTHERN IRELAND WILL FORM 3 - RESIDUE DIRECT TO CHILDREN

PRINT NAME AND ADDRESS
THIS Last Will & Testament is made by me _____

of _____

I REVOKE all previous wills and codicils.

EXECUTORS' NAMES AND ADDRESSES
I APPOINT as executors and trustees of my will

_____ and _____

of _____ of _____

_____ _____

REPLACEMENT EXECUTOR'S NAME AND ADDRESS
and should one or more of them fail to or be unable to act I APPOINT to fill any vacancy

_____

of _____

GUARDIAN'S NAME AND ADDRESS
I APPOINT _____

of _____

to be guardian of any of my children who are minors if my husband/wife dies before me.

SPECIFIC GIFTS AND LEGACIES
I GIVE _____

_____

_____

_____

_____

_____

_____

_____

_____

_____

_____

_____

_____

_____

RESIDUARY GIFT (insert age at which you want your children to inherit capital)

I GIVE the rest of my estate to my executors and trustees to hold on trust to pay my debts, taxes and testamentary expenses and pay the residue to those of my children who survive me and attain the age of _____ years if more than one in equal shares.

PROVIDED THAT if any of my children dies before me or after me but under that age, I GIVE the share that child would have taken to his or her own children who attain 18 equally. If no person shall inherit the residue of my estate under the preceding gifts, I GIVE it to _____

_____

TRUSTEES' POWERS

My trustees shall have the power to apply for the benefit of any beneficiary as my trustees shall in their absolute discretion think fit the whole or any part of the capital to which such beneficiary is or may in the future be entitled.

FUNERAL WISHES

I WISH my body to be ☐ buried ☐ cremated ☐ other instructions _____

_____

DATE

SIGNED by the above-named testator in our presence on the

_____ day of _____ 20 _____

and then by us in the testator's presence

TESTATOR'S SIGNATURE

SIGNED _____

WITNESSES' SIGNATURES NAMES AND ADDRESSES

SIGNED _____ SIGNED _____

_____ _____

of _____ of _____

_____ _____

occupation _____ occupation _____

© 2010 Lawpack Publishing Limited
www.lawpack.co.uk

1003751

Last Will & Testament

SCOTLAND WILL FORM 1 – SIMPLE GIFT OF THE RESIDUE

PRINT FULL NAME AND ADDRESS

THIS Last Will & Testament is made by me _____

of _____

I REVOKE all previous wills and codicils.

EXECUTORS' FULL NAMES AND ADDRESSES

I APPOINT as executors and trustees of my will

name _____ and name _____

of _____ of _____

_____ _____

REPLACEMENT EXECUTOR'S NAME AND ADDRESS

and should one or more of them fail to or be unable to act I APPOINT to fill any vacancy

name _____

of _____

DEBTS AND FUNERAL EXPENSES

I direct my executors to settle my debts and funeral expenses and the expenses of administering my estate;

SPECIFIC GIFTS AND PECUNIARY LEGACIES

I GIVE _____

_____
_____
_____
_____
_____
_____
_____
_____
_____
_____
_____
_____
_____
_____
_____

_____
(Testator's Signature)

RESIDUARY GIFT I GIVE the residue of my estate to _____

_____

_____

but if he/she or (if I have indicated more than one person) any of them fails to survive me by 28 days or if this gift or any part of it fails for any other reason, then I GIVE the residue of my estate or the part of it affected to

_____

EXECUTORS' POWERS And my executors shall have all the powers of gratuitous trustees;

With reference to these presents I HEREBY DECLARE as follows, videlicet:-

That all pecuniary legacies shall be payable without interest and within six months of the date of my death;

That all specific bequests shall be subject to the beneficiary paying the delivery costs;

FUNERAL WISHES I WISH my body to be ☐ buried ☐ cremated ☐ other instructions _____

_____

And in the event of my death, (not survived by my wife/husband),

GUARDIAN'S FULL NAME AND ADDRESS I NOMINATE and APPOINT _____

of _____

to be guardian to such of my children as are under the age of full legal capacity at my death;

DATE IN WITNESS WHEREOF these presents written on this and the preceding page are subscribed by me at

address _____

_____

on the _____ day of _____

_____ before this witness:-

TESTATOR'S SIGNATURE SIGNED _____

WITNESS'S SIGNATURE SIGNED _____

WITNESS'S FULL NAME AND ADDRESS name _____

of _____

_____

occupation _____

© 2010 Lawpack Publishing Limited
www.lawpack.co.uk

1003751

Last Will & Testament

SCOTLAND WILL FORM 2 - RESIDUE TO AN ADULT BUT IF HE/SHE DIES TO CHILDREN

PRINT FULL NAME AND ADDRESS
THIS Last Will & Testament is made by me _____
of _____

I REVOKE all previous wills and codicils.

EXECUTORS' FULL NAMES AND ADDRESSES
I APPOINT as executors and trustees of my will

name _____ and name _____

of _____ of _____

REPLACEMENT EXECUTOR'S NAME AND ADDRESS
and should one or more of them fail to or be unable to act I APPOINT to fill any vacancy

name _____
of _____

DEBTS AND FUNERAL EXPENSES
I direct my executors and trustees to settle my debts and funeral expenses and the expenses of administering my estate;

SPECIFIC GIFTS AND PECUNIARY LEGACIES
I GIVE _____
_____
_____
_____
_____
_____
_____
_____
_____

RESIDUARY GIFT
I GIVE the residue of my estate to _____
_____

(insert age at which you want your children to inherit capital)
but if he/she or (if I have indicated more than one person) any of them fails to survive me by 28 days or if this gift or any part of it fails for any other reason, then I direct my trustees to pay, convey and make over the said residue so far as not disposed of equally between or among or wholly to such of my children as survive the coming into operation of this Clause, and have then attained or thereafter attain the age of _____ years complete, along with the issue who do so survive and attain the said age of any of my children who may fail to so survive or do so survive but fail to attain the said age, such issue taking equally between or among them "per stirpes" if more than one the share of residue, original and accrescing, such as the parent would have taken on survivance;

_____
(Testator's Signature)

TRUSTEES' POWERS
(insert age at which you want your children to inherit capital)

DECLARING that during the minority of any beneficiary hereunder (which for this purpose shall be while such beneficiary is under the age of _____ years complete) who is prospectively entitled to a share of the capital of the said residue in terms of this Clause, my trustees shall apply so much, if any, of the income of the share of capital to which he or she is for the time being prospectively entitled as they in their absolute discretion may from time to time consider to be necessary for his or her maintenance, education or benefit and my trustees shall accumulate so much of the said income as is not applied for the foregoing purposes and add the same to the capital of such share; and

(insert age at which you want your children to become entitled to receive the income)

That on the attainment of the age of _____ years complete of any beneficiary hereunder who is prospectively entitled to a share of the capital of the said residue, my trustees shall, until he or she becomes entitled to receive the said capital, pay to him or her the whole income of the said capital to which he or she is for the time being prospectively entitled and the whole income of any accumulations thereon; and

With reference to these presents I Hereby Declare as follows, videlicet:

That all pecuniary legacies shall be payable without interest and within six months of the date of my death;

That all specific bequests shall be subject to the beneficiary paying the delivery costs;

That no beneficiary shall take a vested interest in any part of the said residue until the term or terms of payment thereof except that all payments or advances which may be made by my trustees by virtue of the powers herein conferred on them shall vest in the beneficiary receiving the same at the date of payment or advance;

That my trustees shall have power in their absolute discretion to advance to any residuary beneficiary hereunder, any part or even the whole of his or her prospective share of the said residue for any purpose which my trustees shall deem to be for his or her permanent advantage or benefit and on such terms and conditions, as my trustees in their uncontrolled discretion think fit;

That my trustees shall have power to pay and make over in whole or in part any funds due or advanced to or on account of any beneficiary under the age of full legal capacity to his or her legal guardian, the receipt of such guardian constituting a sufficient discharge.

That there shall be no apportionment of income between capital and revenue on any occasion, all income being deemed to have accrued at the date upon which it is payable;

And I PROVIDE and DECLARE that my trustees shall have all the powers and immunities of gratuitous trustees and shall not be restricted to investments authorised by the Trustee Investments Act 1961;

FUNERAL WISHES

I WISH my body to be ☐ buried ☐ cremated ☐ other instructions _____

_____

And in the event of my death, (not survived by my wife/husband),

GUARDIAN'S FULL NAME AND ADDRESS

I NOMINATE AND APPOINT _____

of _____

to be the guardian to such of my children as are under the age of full legal capacity at my death;

DATE

IN WITNESS WHEREOF these presents written on this and the preceding page are subscribed by me at

address _____

on the _____ day of _____

_____ before this witness:

TESTATOR'S SIGNATURE

SIGNED _____

WITNESS'S SIGNATURE

SIGNED _____

WITNESS'S FULL NAME AND ADDRESS

name _____

of _____

_____

occupation _____

© 2010 Lawpack Publishing Limited
www.lawpack.co.uk

1003751

Last Will & Testament

SCOTLAND WILL FORM 3 - RESIDUE DIRECT TO CHILDREN

PRINT FULL NAME AND ADDRESS

THIS Last Will & Testament is made by me _____

of _____

I REVOKE all previous wills and codicils.

EXECUTORS' FULL NAMES AND ADDRESSES

I APPOINT as executors and trustees of my will

name _____ and name _____

of _____ of _____

_____ _____

REPLACEMENT EXECUTOR'S NAME AND ADDRESS

and should one or more of them fail to or be unable to act I APPOINT to fill any vacancy

name _____

of _____

DEBTS AND FUNERAL EXPENSES

I direct my executors and trustees to settle my debts and funeral expenses and the expenses of administering my estate;

SPECIFIC GIFTS AND PECUNIARY LEGACIES

I GIVE _____

_____

_____

_____

_____

_____

_____

_____

_____

_____

_____

_____

_____

RESIDUARY GIFT

(insert age at which you want your children to inherit capital)

I direct my trustees to pay, convey and make over the residue of my estate equally between or among or wholly to such of my children as survive the coming into operation of this Clause, and have then attained or thereafter attain the age of _____ years complete, along with the issue who do so survive and attain the said age of any of my children who may fail to so survive or do so survive but fail to attain the said age, such issue taking equally between or among them "per stirpes" if more than one the share of residue, original and accrescing, such as the parent would have taken on survivance;

_____

(Testator's Signature)

TRUSTEES' POWERS
(insert age at which you want your children to inherit capital)

DECLARING that during the minority of any beneficiary hereunder (which for this purpose shall be while such beneficiary is under the age of ____ years complete) who is prospectively entitled to a share of the capital of the said residue in terms of this Clause, my trustees shall apply so much, if any, of the income of the share of capital to which he or she is for the time being prospectively entitled as they in their absolute discretion may from time to time consider to be necessary for his or her maintenance, education or benefit and my trustees shall accumulate so much of the said income as is not applied for the foregoing purposes and add the same to the capital of such share; and

(insert age at which you want your children to become entitled to receive the income)

That on the attainment of the age of ____ years complete of any beneficiary hereunder who is prospectively entitled to a share of the capital of the said residue, my trustees shall, until he or she becomes entitled to receive the said capital, pay to him or her the whole income of the said capital to which he or she is for the time being prospectively entitled and the whole income of any accumulations thereon; and

With reference to these presents I Hereby Declare as follows, videlicet:

That all pecuniary legacies shall be payable without interest and within six months of the date of my death;

That all specific bequests shall be subject to the beneficiary paying the delivery costs;

That no beneficiary shall take a vested interest in any part of the said residue until the term or terms of payment thereof except that all payments or advances which may be made by my trustees by virtue of the powers herein conferred on them shall vest in the beneficiary receiving the same at the date of payment or advance;

That my trustees shall have power in their absolute discretion to advance to any residuary beneficiary hereunder, any part or even the whole of his or her prospective share of the said residue for any purpose which my trustees shall deem to be for his or her permanent advantage or benefit and on such terms and conditions, as my trustees in their uncontrolled discretion think fit;

That my trustees shall have power to pay and make over in whole or in part any funds due or advanced to or on account of any beneficiary under the age of full legal capacity to his or her legal guardian, the receipt of such guardian constituting a sufficient discharge.

That there shall be no apportionment of income between capital and revenue on any occasion, all income being deemed to have accrued at the date upon which it is payable;

And I PROVIDE and DECLARE that my trustees shall have all the powers and immunities of gratuitous trustees and shall not be restricted to investments authorised by the Trustee Investments Act 1961;

FUNERAL WISHES

I WISH my body to be ☐ buried ☐ cremated ☐ other instructions _____
_____

And in the event of my death, (not survived by my wife/husband),

GUARDIAN'S FULL NAME AND ADDRESS

I NOMINATE AND APPOINT _____

of _____

to be guardian to such of my children as are under the age of full legal capacity at my death;

DATE

IN WITNESS WHEREOF these presents written on this and the preceding page are subscribed by me at

address _____

on the _____ day of _____

_____ before this witness:

TESTATOR'S SIGNATURE

SIGNED _____

WITNESS'S SIGNATURE

SIGNED _____

WITNESS'S FULL NAME AND ADDRESS

name _____

of _____

_____

occupation _____

© 2010 Lawpack Publishing Limited
www.lawpack.co.uk

1003751

Get the most out of your Will Kit

With **Updates & Downloads** you can obtain:*

- ✔ Extra Will Forms*
- ✔ Letter to Executor template*
- ✔ Important Document Locator*
- ✔ Funeral Wishes template*
- ✔ Property Inventory*
- ✔ Guide for Executors as eBook
- ✔ Information on law changes

How do I access my Updates & Downloads?

By following these three simple steps you will be taken to the **Updates & Downloads** section of the Lawpack site, where you will then be able to download any extra content associated with your Will Kit.

1 Type the following web address into your internet browser's address bar:

www.lawpack.co.uk/P130

The illustrations below show two of the most popular browsers with their address bars shown.

Internet Explorer

Type the web address here

Firefox

Type the web address here

2 You will then be taken to the **Updates & Downloads** section for your Will Kit. To access the forms, enter the following code into the registration code box and click **Activate**:

P1301012799

3 You will now have access to the documents, as well as information on any minor legal changes that affect the Will Kit.

* Documents in Microsoft Word

Security and peace of mind for you and your family

Lawpack Will Storage

12 MONTHS' FREE WILL STORAGE WORTH £12.00

The original copy of your Will is an important document and needs to be stored securely. You may have thought of storing it at home - but what if it becomes lost or is stolen? And would it remain completely confidential? Storing your Will with a local solicitor or bank could be the answer, but this may be inconvenient and costly. And if you move out of the area, how would your executors know where to find it?

Lawpack's Will Storage Service offers you a simple and secure solution, giving complete protection to your Will with no time limit.

- Using Lawpack's Will Storage Service your Will will be stored at Lawpack's fire-proof, secure storage facility.
- Your Will is held in a sealed envelope with a unique barcode, so that it can be retrieved instantly. If you need to make changes, your Will can be despatched to you within two working days, by post.
- With your consent, we inform your executors where your Will is stored and make sure that only he or she can retrieve it after death.
- If you instruct us to do so, we can inform your chosen charities about bequests or legacies included in your Will. Charities appreciate this service.

With your first year's storage **FREE** (and subsequently £12.00 a year), we will store your Will, giving you the peace of mind of knowing that your last wishes are in safe hands.

How to apply

Apply today by telephone, email, online or by post, quoting '**Free Will Storage**'. You will then receive your comprehensive Will Storage Pack, containing full instructions, and storage envelope.

Tel: 020 7394 4040
Email: will-storage@lawpack.co.uk
Online: www.lawpack.co.uk/willstorage
Address: Lawpack Will Storage, 76-89 Alscot Road, London, SE1 3AW

Do-it-yourself Will Kit

LAWPACK

Guide for Executors

In association with Irwin Mitchell Solicitors

irwinmitchell solicitors

Lawpack Publishing Limited
76–89 Alscot Road
London SE1 3AW

www.lawpack.co.uk

All rights reserved
Printed in Great Britain

© 2011 Lawpack Publishing Limited

This Lawpack Guide may not be reproduced in whole or in part in any form without written permission from the publisher.

Note:
- Since 2005, it has been possible for same-sex partners to register their relationships, so becoming 'registered civil partners'. For many purposes, and for most of the rules related to Wills and intestacy, registered civil partners are treated in the same way as spouses. Throughout this guide, for 'spouse' read 'spouse or civil partner'.
- This guide is for use in England & Wales and Scotland only. The law is stated as at 1 January 2011.
- Figures are quoted for the tax year 2010/2011.
- For convenience (and for no other reason) 'him', 'he' and 'his' have been used throughout and should be read to include 'her', 'she' and 'her'.

Exclusion of liability and disclaimer

While every effort has been made to ensure that this Lawpack publication provides accurate and expert guidance, it is impossible to predict all the circumstances in which it may be used. Accordingly, neither the publisher, author, retailer, approving solicitors, nor any other suppliers shall be liable to any person or entity with respect to any loss or damage caused or alleged to be caused by the information contained in or omitted from this Lawpack publication.

Contents

1. What is an executor?	5
Grant of probate or confirmation	5
More than one executor	5
Other personal representatives	5
Should a solicitor be instructed?	7
2. When death occurs	7
Registering the death	7
The death certificate	8
The Will	8
3. Duties of an executor	9
Is a grant of probate or confirmation necessary?	10
Financial records	11
Paying Inheritance Tax	11
Identifying beneficiaries	11
4. Taking stock	12
Valuing debts	12
Asset checklist	12
House or flat	12
Bank account	13
Stocks and shares	13
Businesses	14
Car	14
Jewellery	14
Works of art	14
Other possessions	14
National Savings	14
Premium Bonds	14
Outstanding salary or pension payments	14
Life insurance and pension policies	15
Taxes and bills	15
Social Security payments	15
Foreign property	15
5. Applying for a grant	15
Excepted/exempt estates	15
The forms – England and Wales	16
Form PA1 Probate Application Form	16
Form IHT 205 Short Form of Return of estate information	17
Form IHT 400 Inheritance Tax Account	17

The forms – Scotland	17
Form C1 Confirmation	17
Form C5 (SE) Information about Small Estates	17
Form C5 Short Form of Return of estate information	17
Form IHT 400	19
Bond of caution	19
Application for confirmation – Scotland	19
The forms – England, Wales & Scotland	19
Form IHT 400 Full Inheritance Tax Return	19
Schedules Form IHT 411 & Form IHT 412 Stocks and Shares	20
Schedule IHT 405 Houses, land, buildings and interests in land	20
At the Probate Registry – England & Wales	20
At the Sheriff Court – Scotland	20
Inheritance tax	21
Changes to the amount of Inheritance Tax	21
Raising money to pay Inheritance Tax and the probate fee or confirmation dues	21
6. Administering an estate	**22**
Distribution of gifts and legacies	22
Transfer of assets	22
Final accounts	23
Taxation of the estate	23
Succession on intestacy	24
The rules of intestacy in England and Wales	24
Prior rights, legal rights and the rules of intestacy in Scotland	26
7. An overview of probate/confirmation	**29**

What is an executor?

When someone is named the executor of a Will, he is being asked to take responsibility for administering the estate of the person who made the Will, called the testator, upon the testator's death.

Acting as an executor should not be undertaken lightly. Immediately following the death, the executors are expected to begin their administrative duties; long after other mourners' lives have returned to normal, the executors will still be administering the estate. This entails corresponding with other parties, keeping meticulous records, filling out forms and being answerable to creditors, beneficiaries and the intentions of the deceased, as recorded in the Will.

Don't be put off by the term 'estate'. This simply refers to all the property a person leaves behind, whether its value be hundreds or millions of pounds. One person's assets may include homes, yachts and a Swiss bank account, while another leaves a wedding ring, some changes of clothes and a shoe box full of costume jewellery. Both have left estates to be accounted for and distributed.

Executors' duties can be summed up as: taking an inventory of the deceased's possessions and debts, collecting the assets, paying the bills and distributing the legacies (whether specific items, cash sums or residue) following the testator's wishes as closely as possible.

The following sections take you through the probate process in England and Wales or the process in Scotland, without the services of a solicitor.

Grant of probate or confirmation

Executors have the power to deal with the deceased's assets from the date of death, but not until they receive what is called in England and Wales a 'grant of probate', or in Scotland 'confirmation', can they prove their authority to those institutions and authorities that hold assets in the deceased's name. In England and Wales, grants of probate are issued by the High Court through Probate Registries. In Scotland, confirmation is issued by the Commissary Department of the Sheriff Court in the area where the deceased had been domiciled at death.

More than one executor

If the Will appoints only one executor, or if only one person is able and willing to act, a grant of probate or confirmation can be issued to one person. In England and Wales, if the Will appoints more than four executors, only four of them will be allowed to apply for the grant of probate. The others may renounce their right to apply for probate; or they may decide not to apply for the time being but to reserve their right to apply in the future so that if, for example, one of the acting executors dies before the estate has been fully administered, the executor with power reserved may take his place.

In England and Wales, if only one executor is taking out the grant of probate, it may be prudent for the other executor(s) to sign what's called a 'power reserved' letter, even if it's not anticipated that he will want to apply at any stage. By reserving the right to apply in this way, a non-acting executor can step in if the acting executor becomes incapacitated before the administration of the estate is complete. The Probate Registry provides a form necessary to renounce or reserve the right to apply for probate.

In Scotland, there is no limit on the number of executors who may be appointed under a Will, but for practical reasons, it is probably not desirable to have more than four. Confirmation is always issued in favour of all surviving executors who have been nominated and who haven't predeceased the deceased or declined office. There is no Scottish equivalent to the English and Welsh power reserved option and any executor named in the Will but not wishing to have confirmation issued in his favour, must sign a 'declinature' to be submitted to the Sheriff Court with the application for confirmation.

No matter how many executors are named, for practical purposes it's usually easier if one of the executors undertakes the administrative tasks on behalf of them all (he is referred to in this guide as the 'first applicant'). The executors should meet to discuss the practical side of carrying out their duties. Whatever is agreed should be put in writing and signed by them all. In fact, all official paperwork may need to be signed by all executors, even if they agree that one of them is the first applicant (the exception being that in Scotland the application for confirmation [Form C1] needs to be signed by only one executor).

Caution: If it looks as though the deceased's estate is insolvent, i.e. the debts of the deceased and other liabilities of the estate, including funeral expenses, will exceed the value of the assets in the estate, executors should think carefully before applying for the grant of probate or confirmation and should seek professional legal advice.

Other personal representatives

If an executor renounces the right to take out the grant of probate or in Scotland if a nominated executor declines to accept office, any substitute executor named in the Will steps in and proceeds to apply for the grant of probate or confirmation. If no executor is named in the Will or if the executor named cannot or doesn't wish to act and no substitute is named, beneficiaries can apply to act as the deceased's personal representatives. A beneficiary acting as the testator's personal representative is, in England and Wales, known as the 'administrator' and the grant itself is called a 'grant of letters of administration with Will annexed'.

An administrator's duties are essentially the same as those of an executor. This guide refers to executors, but the rights and responsibilities of both are the same in most respects, whether the person doing the work is an executor or an administrator.

In England and Wales, beneficiaries may apply for a grant as the deceased's administrators in the following order of priority:

1. Any residuary beneficiary.
2. Any personal representative of a residuary beneficiary.
3. Any other 'legatee' (i.e. someone who receives a legacy).
4. Any personal representative of any other legatee.
5. Any creditor.

In Scotland, an executor appointed in terms of a Will is called an 'executor-nominate' and an executor appointed by the Court is called an 'executor-dative' (appropriate where there is no Will and the deceased died 'intestate' or where there is a Will but not all assets have been disposed of, thus creating a 'partial intestacy'). Where there is a Will but no executor has been named, or there is no surviving executor who agrees to accept office, it is still possible to have an executor-nominate appointed if certain conditions can be met. The Sheriff Clerk at the relevant Sheriff Court will be able to advise. The order of priority to be appointed executor-nominate is:

1. Any trustees appointed under the Will to administer a trust created by the Will.
2. A 'general disponee', 'universal legatory', or 'residuary legatee' – all terms meaning the person or persons entitled to the residue of the estate.

If the conditions to obtain a nominate appointment cannot be met, it will be necessary to submit a petition to the Court for the appointment of an executor-dative. The order of priority to be appointed executor-dative follows the order of entitlement to succession to the intestate estate which is set out on page 26.

In England and Wales, a minor (someone under the age of 18) may not act as an executor. If a minor is the only executor appointed in a Will, his parents or guardian are entitled to take out a grant of letters of administration with Will annexed on his behalf. The minor has the right to apply for the grant of probate on attaining his 18th birthday, if the administration of the estate has not been completed.

In Scotland, a person reaching 16 years old has legal capacity and in principle, may act as executor, however, there can be practical difficulties and it is not recommended that a person below the age of 18 be appointed executor. Where a child below the age of 16 has been named as executor and has parents or a guardian, the parents/guardian may seek appointment and be confirmed as executor on behalf of the child, or may decline office on the child's behalf.

If the deceased left no Will, he is said to have died 'intestate' and the estate is distributed in accordance with the rules of intestacy. In England and Wales, the personal representatives are, again, known as administrators and the grant is called a 'grant of letters of administration'. In Scotland, the personal representatives are, when appointed, known as executors-dative but the grant is still known as confirmation. In England and Wales, when there is no Will, administrators are appointed in the following order of priority:

1. The deceased's spouse.
2. Any child of the deceased and any issue of a child who died before the deceased.
3. The parents of the deceased.
4. Brothers and sisters of the whole blood of the deceased and the issue of any who died before the deceased.
5. Brothers and sisters of the half blood of the deceased and the issue of any who died before the deceased.
6. Grandparents of the deceased.
7. Uncles and aunts of the whole blood and the issue of any who died before the deceased.
8. Uncles and aunts of the half blood and the issue of any who died before the deceased.

In England and Wales, the maximum number of administrators is four, whether there is a Will or the person died intestate. A sole administrator may take out the grant only where none of the beneficiaries is under 18 or where no life interest arises. If either of these is the case, the grant must issue to a minimum of two administrators.

In England and Wales, a life interest most commonly arises where the deceased's estate is worth more than £250,000 and he died intestate leaving a spouse and a child or children. In that case, the spouse will take the first £250,000 as a legacy, all the personal chattels, and will have a life interest in half of the residue of the estate: the remaining half of the estate is held in trust for the child or children until reaching 18; they also benefit from the spouse's life interest on his death.

In Scotland, where there is no Will, or there is a partial intestacy, it is necessary for an executor-dative to be appointed. An executor-dative is appointed on application to the Sheriff Court in the area where the deceased had been domiciled at the date of his death. That application is by way of petition in prescribed form.

Historically, the order of priority to be appointed executor-dative is:

1. A general disponee, universal legatory or residuary legatee (only relevant where there is a Will naming beneficiaries but giving rise to a partial intestacy).
2. The 'next of kin'. This term means the surviving members of the class of relatives nearest in degree to the deceased, related through the father's line. This would exclude the deceased's spouse, mother and any maternal relations.
3. The deceased's creditors.
4. 'Special legatees', i.e. those entitled to a legacy of a specific item of estate rather than a residuary legatee (again, only relevant where there is a Will but a partial intestacy arises).

However, contemporary Sheriff Court practice is that the

person or persons entitled to receive the deceased's estate under the rules of intestate succession (which post date the creation of the above order of preference) will be found entitled to the office of executor-dative. The same legislation provides that the surviving spouse has the right – treated in practice as the exclusive right – to the office of executor-dative, where he is entitled to the whole of the intestate estate under the succession rules. In Scotland, in an intestate estate no 'liferent' (or life interest) arises – the Scottish rules of intestate succession are explained on page 26.

Should a solicitor be instructed?

Executors can instruct a solicitor, stockbroker or other adviser to perform specific duties even if they do not use a solicitor to make the probate or confirmation application. Whether an executor handles all the tasks involved in administering the estate or uses professional advisers is a matter of choice and convenience. Any fees properly incurred are paid out of the estate.

This *Guide for Executors* is designed to help the layperson sort out a simple, straightforward Will or intestacy. If the Will or the estate is complex, a solicitor should be consulted. If you are in any doubt, seek professional advice. Some signs that a solicitor should be involved include the following:

1. The estate is insolvent.
2. A beneficiary cannot be contacted.
3. Someone intends to challenge the Will.
4. There is some question of the Will's validity, or the Will cannot be found.
5. Someone stands to inherit a life interest in, or liferent of, the estate.
6. Beneficiaries include children under the age of 18 (in Scotland, 16) and a trust is set up for them.
7. The deceased owned a business or was a partner in a business or owned agricultural property.
8. The deceased was a Name (i.e. an investor) in Lloyd's of London insurance market.
9. A trust is set up under the Will.
10. Any house or land in the estate has an unregistered title.
11. The Inheritance Tax calculations are particularly complex.
12. One or more beneficiaries wish to vary the terms of the Will in so far as it affects their entitlement.
13. There is no Will but a cohabitee neither married to, nor in a civil partnership with the deceased, may wish to make a claim on the intestate estate.

If you need specific assistance from a solicitor or would like to see how a solicitor can help to administer the estate, national law firm Irwin Mitchell Solicitors have significant experience and expertise in the provision of estate administration, probate and confirmation advice, including advice on estate disputes and conveyancing of estate properties.

Irwin Mitchell can be contacted on 0845 604 1722. Please quote reference 'Lawpack Executors'.

When death occurs

When someone dies, a doctor should be called. He will issue a medical certificate stating the cause or causes of death, along with a notice setting out who is eligible to register the death with the local Registrar of Births and Deaths.

Registering the death

In England and Wales, if the death has occurred inside a house or public building, the following people may act as informant, in the following order:

1. A relative of the deceased who was present at the death.
2. A relative of the deceased who was present during the final stages of the illness.
3. A relative of the deceased who lives in the district where the death occurred.
4. Anyone who was present at the death.
5. Someone in authority in the building where the death occurred who was aware of the circumstances of the death; for example, the owner of a nursing home or the warden of sheltered accommodation.
6. Any resident of the building where the death occurred, if he was aware of the circumstances of the death.
7. The person who accepts responsibility for arranging the funeral.

If the death occurred outside a house or public building, the follow¬ing people are eligible to register the death in the following order:

1. A relative of the deceased able to provide the Registrar with the necessary details.
2. Anyone who was present at the death.
3. The person who found the body.
4. The person in charge of the body (the police if the body is unidentified).
5. The person who accepts responsibility for arranging the funeral.

In Scotland, the death must be registered by:

1. Any relative of the deceased.
2. Any person present at the death.

3. The executor or other legal representative of the deceased.
4. The occupier at the time of death of the premises where the death occurred.
5. If there is no person as above, any other person having knowledge of the particulars to be registered.

In England and Wales, within five days, or in Scotland within eight days, of the death, the informant must take the medical certificate to the Registrar of Deaths, or must send written notice. In England and Wales, the deceased's medical card should be given to the Registrar as well. The Registrar will ask for other details about the deceased:

1. The date and place of death (birth certificate should be produced if available).
2. The full name of the deceased, including any maiden name.
3. The date and place of birth of the deceased.
4. The occupation of the deceased.
5. The name, date of birth and occupation of the deceased's spouse (and in Scotland, former spouses), whether or not still living.
6. The deceased's usual address.
7. Whether the deceased received any state pension or allowance.
8. The date of birth of any surviving spouse.
9. In Scotland, the full names and occupations of the parents of the deceased should also be provided (if known).

The death certificate

Once the death has been registered, the informant will be given a death certificate, which is a copy of the entry on the register (and in Scotland, also (1) a certificate for the funeral director dealing with the funeral, (2) a free abbreviated death certificate and (3) a Social Security notification of death form to assist in obtaining or adjusting benefits). There is a small charge for each copy of the full death certificate, and it's sensible to get three or four copies. The executors may need to send copies to the deceased's bank, to the registrars of companies in which he held shares, to insurance companies holding policies written in trust and, in England and Wales, to the Probate Registry. Although you can have the certificate returned to you once it has been inspected, it may be more convenient to circulate several copies at once.

Note: A while after the death the cost of a copy of the death certificate may increase. The period varies depending on the register office so it's worth checking if it's probable further copies will be needed.

The Will

If the executors are prepared for their duties, they may have been in possession of a copy of the Will even before the death and know the location of the original. They may know of the deceased's instructions concerning organ donation, disposal of the body and funeral wishes. All of this information is needed in the first hours following death.

Arranging the funeral is not specifically the duty of executors and should be handled by whoever is most aware of the deceased's wishes. But anyone who manages the funeral is entitled to have the account settled out of money from the estate.

If there is no opportunity for preparation before the death, the Will must be located to determine who has been named its executor(s). If no Will is found at the deceased's home, it may have been sent to his bank or solicitor for safekeeping or to Lawpack's Will Storage Service. In England and Wales, it may have been deposited at the Principal Registry (formerly Somerset House), in which case a deposit certificate will have been issued on receipt of the Will; the Will can be reclaimed by sending the certificate to:

Record Keeper's Department
Principal Registry of the Family Division
First Avenue House
42–49 High Holborn
London WC1V 6NP
Tel: 020 7947 7022

If a Will is found, ascertain that it is the deceased's last Will by making enquiries at, for example, the deceased's bank and solicitor. It must bear the signature of the deceased (in Scotland, it must be signed on every page) and of an appropriate witness or witnesses.

In England and Wales, probate may be granted on a copy, but you should notify the Probate Registry as soon as possible that the original cannot be found. The Registry will tell you what evidence is needed as proof that the original Will had not been revoked by being destroyed before death.

In Scotland, if only a copy of the signed Will can be found, it may possible for the executors to treat the estate as testate and proceed to wind up the estate in accordance with the copy Will but it will be necessary in the first instance to raise an action in the Court of Session in Edinburgh to 'prove the tenor' of the original signed Will using the copy. If this fails, the estate must be treated as intestate and wound up accordingly.

The necessity of a formal 'reading of the Will' before hopeful beneficiaries, or a solicitor, is a myth. There is no legal requirement for any such reading but it is courteous to write to beneficiaries to inform them of their entitlement under the Will.

There may be some doubt as to who the beneficiaries are under the Will. Many Wills describe certain beneficiaries in terms of groups of people, for example 'my children,' rather than naming them. The expression 'my children' includes, by law, children conceived at the time of the deceased's death and subsequently born alive, adopted children and, in England and Wales, legitimated children (children born to unmarried parents who later marry). In

Scotland, illegitimate children (i.e. children born outside marriage) are also included in the expression 'my children'.

In England and Wales, if the Will was executed after 3rd April 1988, children whose parents were married to each other at the time of their birth are treated in the same way as those whose parents were not, even if the executors have no knowledge of the children's existence. If the Will was executed before then, the executors will not be liable to a testator's child born outside marriage if they didn't know of his existence. These rules apply unless it is clear from the Will that the deceased intended otherwise.

In Scotland, if the Will was executed on or after 25 November 1968, in determining who should be the beneficiaries of an estate, no distinction is to be drawn between legitimate and illegitimate relationships. This applies to all relationships including the construction of such terms as grandchildren, brother, cousin, etc. These rules apply unless it is clear from the Will that the deceased intended otherwise.

For Wills executed in Scotland prior to that date, the common law continues to apply and expressions such as 'children' or 'issue' are presumed to refer to legitimate relationships only, unless the Will indicates otherwise. Providing the executor is acting in good faith having made all reasonable enquiries, statute gives the executor some protection, allowing him to distribute the estate without instigating an exhaustive search for potential illegitimate claimants or any person adopted by the deceased who would also have a claim on the estate.

Generally, if a beneficiary named in a Will has died before the testator, the gift to him will simply not take effect. However, if that beneficiary is a child, grandchild or great-grandchild or remoter issue of the testator (or in Scotland, a nephew or niece of the testator, but the extension of the principle is limited to those specific relatives only), and he has left children of his own, the children step into or may step into their parent's shoes and their entitlement under the Will, shared equally between them.

In England and Wales (but not in Scotland), if the deceased married after making the Will and the Will was not expressed to be in expectation of the marriage, the Will is automatically revoked. Divorce, however, does not revoke a Will, but in England and Wales (but not in Scotland), the former spouse is treated as if he died on the date of the divorce so that he cannot take a gift under the Will or act as an executor.

In Scotland, it should be noted that the legal rights of the spouse and issue of the deceased, apply even in testate cases and these entitlements can affect the division of the estate, regardless of the terms of a Will – see page 26. The executors must deal with this issue as part of the administration of a testate estate.

If the executors are uncertain as to the interpretation of other parts of the Will, they should seek the advice of a solicitor to avoid the risk of distributing the money wrongly.

Once probate or confirmation is granted the Will becomes a public document, but until then the beneficiaries may know nothing of their legacies, unless the deceased told them before he died. However, the executors will usually tell the beneficiaries that they have been left a legacy, although it's impossible to be specific about the amount if it's a legacy of residue or part of residue. But no legacy can be guaranteed at this stage as the Will may be found invalid, may be challenged, or the assets of the estate may not be sufficient to pay all the legacies.

Duties of an executor

In preparation for dealing with the assets and liabilities of the estate, some administrative tasks should be attended to by the executors as soon as possible.

Have the deceased's postal address changed to that of the first applicant, the executor who is to handle day-to-day business and personal affairs. If the home is to be left unoccupied, the executors should ensure that it's securely locked; that water, electricity and gas supplies have been turned off and mail redirected.

The executors should also ensure that there are both current buildings and contents insurance policies on the home. The executors may be held liable by any beneficiary who receives less from the estate than he should have because of a burglary, fire or other loss. The insurers should be notified of the death and given the names and addresses of the executors. If there are particularly valuable items at the deceased's home and it's to be left unoccupied, it may be better to remove them for safekeeping.

Finally, the executors should open an executors' bank account into which they will eventually deposit the proceeds of assets and from which they will pay the bills of the deceased.

Make a thorough search of the deceased's papers and online records for the documents that will be needed to finalise the deceased's affairs. These will include:

- Cheque books
- Bank statements
- Savings certificates and other national savings assets
- Outstanding bills
- Share certificates and stockbroker's details
- Car registration documents
- Mortgage papers
- Insurance and pension documentation
- Information on jewellery and collectables; for example, insurance valuations
- Tax assessments, returns and other tax papers

The executors' aims are to:

1. Identify the assets of the estate and assess their value at date of death.

2. Identify the deceased's debts and pay them.
3. Distribute the legacies.

Is a grant of probate or confirmation necessary?

Whilst itemising the assets of the estate, the executors must bear in mind that it may not be necessary to apply for a grant of probate (England and Wales) or for confirmation (Scotland). Whether or not a grant is required depends not only on the size of the deceased's estate, but also on the kinds of assets in it. Normally, a grant is required where the value of the deceased's estate (after paying the funeral account) exceeds £5,000. The grant vests authority in the executors to deal with the estate. Without that authority, the executors would be relying solely on the validity of the Will.

For example, if the deceased only left a great deal of cash, personal items having a high market value and a very expensive car, there is no need to apply for a grant of probate or confirmation because executors need no formal proof of their authority to gather in and distribute such assets. On the other hand, if the deceased had a bank account and shares with a net value of over £5,000, or if the deceased's home needs to be sold or transferred to a beneficiary, a grant will be necessary so the executors can obtain formal authority to gather in and deal with these assets.

Certain authorities can pay sums due on death to the person entitled under a Will or intestacy without requiring sight of a grant of probate, as long as the amount payable is (normally) less than £5,000. The assets concerned include:

- **National Savings, including prizes won on Premium Bonds.** In order to claim, the executors need to complete Form NSA 904, which is available from post offices, and send it to the address given on that form for the type of account held, together with a registrar's copy of the death certificate.
- **Building society accounts, deposits with friendly societies, trade union deposits of members, arrears of salary or pension due to government or local government employees and police and firemen's pensions.** The executors should write to the relevant authority, asking for a claim form and sending a registrar's copy of the death certificate.

Other assets that may be realised without the executors needing to produce the grant of probate or confirmation are:

- **Nominated property.** Until 1981, the holder of certain National Savings investments and government stock could nominate someone to receive them on his death. After 1981, no new nominations could be made, but those made before that year are valid. Such a nomination takes effect independently of the deceased's Will or intestacy and independently of any grant of probate. The person nominated can have such stocks transferred into his name or redeemed on producing the death certificate. There is no upper limit on the value of the nominated property which can be dealt with in this way, but if the institution is concerned that the estate may be large enough for Inheritance Tax (IHT) to be paid on it, it may require the executors to obtain a certificate from HM Revenue & Customs (HMRC) to show that any such tax has been paid.
- **Jointly held assets.** When two people hold property jointly (as joint tenants in England and Wales, or in Scotland where there is a specific or implied survivorship destination), on the death of one of them, his share of the asset passes directly to the other by right of survivorship, regardless of the provisions of the Will or the intestacy rules. Such assets might include a house or flat, or bank or building society accounts. No grant of probate or confirmation is required to transfer the deceased's share of these assets to the surviving joint holder. If the property is a house or flat, and in England and Wales the land is registered land, a registrar's copy of the death certificate should be sent to the Land Registry to enable the survivor to be registered as the sole surviving owner of the house or flat. In England and Wales, if the land is unregistered land, a registrar's copy of the death certificate should be kept with the title deeds and will need to be produced when the land is sold. In Scotland, with property where there is a survivorship destination, no action is required (whether or not the property is registered in the Land Registry of Scotland) except that a copy of the death certificate should be held as part of the surviving owner's title. If the joint asset is a bank or building society account, a registrar's copy of the death certificate should be sent to the relevant bank or building society so the deceased's name may be removed from the account. Therefore, if the deceased's estate consists solely of jointly held assets, there would normally be no need for the executors to apply for a grant of probate or confirmation.

However, in Scotland, where one person opens a bank or building society account in joint names, unless it is specified at the outset that they are actually making a gift to the joint account holder, the fact that there is a joint account holder is significant only for the bank's administrative purposes. The bank may well automatically transfer the account after death to the joint account holder, but this does not mean that the joint holder is necessarily entitled to the whole account. The entitlement to the account (and therefore the proportion attributable to the deceased) will depend upon the proportions in which each account holder contributed to and made withdrawals from the account. It may ultimately be necessary to recover some funds from the joint account holder to meet claims on the deceased's estate and satisfy bequests in the Will.

Probate or confirmation forms

In England and Wales, the Probate Registry will supply the

executors with the required forms, but it's best to ask for them early on in the probate process. In Scotland, the Sheriff Clerk's Office of the Sheriff Court in the area where the deceased had been domiciled at death will supply the executors with the required forms. As the inventory and valuation process progresses, executors can fill in the forms as they go along.

A note on Probate Registries in England and Wales: all executors will need to make at least one visit to the Probate Registry or a local office (not so in Scotland). In dealing with an estate in England and Wales, apart from the Principal Registry in London, there are district Registries and local offices under their control throughout the country. It's sensible to choose a Registry or local office conveniently located for the executors; bear in mind that some local offices do have minimal and sporadic office hours which may not necessarily result in a quick or convenient service, and that not all Probate Registries have identical procedures.

Financial records

During the administration of the estate, the executors must keep track of every financial transaction, no matter how small. The money and assets belonging to the estate must be kept entirely separate from the executors' personal money and assets. Out-of-pocket expenses of the executors should be recorded as carefully as the payment of bank and probate fees or confirmation dues or Inheritance Taxes.

Although executors are paid for their efforts only if the Will so specifies, expenses the executors incur, such as postage, travel costs, telephone bills, etc., can be paid from the estate.

More importantly, the executors must be able to account for every penny of the testator's estate. They have a fiduciary responsibility (i.e. one of trust) to the creditors and beneficiaries of the estate. When the estate has been fully administered, the executors will need to draw up accounts to demonstrate to the beneficiaries how the assets of the estate were spent or distributed.

Paying Inheritance Tax

Once a thorough valuation of the deceased's assets and liabilities is completed, any Inheritance Tax due must be paid before applying for the grant of probate or confirmation. However, few financial institutions will hand over the funds of the deceased until there is a grant of probate or confirmation to prove the executors' authority.

If the deceased had funds in a National Savings account or held National Savings Certificates and Premium Bonds, National Savings may issue a cheque in favour of HMRC to cover all or part of the tax, thereby permitting the grant of probate or confirmation. Similar arrangements may be made between a building society account and HM Revenue & Customs. Other banks may be willing to arrange a loan to the executors to pay the Inheritance Tax, thereby releasing the funds to repay the loan.

As an alternative to the above, it may be possible to arrange for the tax to be paid direct from the account in the deceased's sole name in a bank or building society, using HMRC form D20. You will need to obtain a tax reference from HMRC for the estate. When you are ready to apply for probate, send the D20 to the bank or building society and they will pay HMRC direct from the account.

Identifying beneficiaries

Once the liabilities of the estate have been paid, the executors identify the beneficiaries of the estate: either those named in the Will or those entitled under the intestacy rules. If the executors distribute the estate incorrectly, they are personally liable to the rightful beneficiaries and to creditors about whom they know or should have known.

In England and Wales, to protect themselves from unknown creditors and beneficiaries, the executors can follow a statutory procedure which involves the placing of advertisements for creditors in the *London Gazette* at:

London Gazette
PO Box 7923
London SE1 5ZH
www.london-gazette.co.uk
Tel: 0870 600 33 22

Executors must also advertise in a newspaper circulating in the area where the deceased lived and, particularly if he owned a business, the area where he worked at the time of death. If land is to be distributed, an advertisement should also be placed in a newspaper circulating in the district where the land is situated.

The advertisements should state that anyone with a claim against or an interest in the estate must make their claim known within a stated time (not less than two months) from the date of the notice, after which the executors may distribute the estate, having regard only to those claims of which they have notice. After the stated time, in England and Wales, anyone who has not come forward cannot make a claim against the executors, although they may claim against the beneficiaries of the estate into whose hands assets have passed.

Advertising for unknown creditors may not be necessary if there is no reason to suspect that the deceased has incurred debts other than those known to the executor. In Scotland, there is no statutory requirement to advertise for creditors, but the executors may consider this prudent, depending upon the level of information in relation to the deceased and his personal circumstances.

Note: Unlike an executor, an administrator in England and Wales can place statutory advertisements only after the grant of letters of administration has been issued.

Taking stock

As a first step, the executors should list those assets which they know, based on personal observation or findings, the deceased owned. This guide includes a checklist below which sets out the most commonly owned assets.

Following this inventory by observation, the executor sends notification of the death to the deceased's bank, building society, accountant, insurance company and other institutions. The letters to the bank and building society should request information about each account and instruct them to stop all unpaid cheques and standing orders. Also ask for a list of deeds and other documents held on behalf of the deceased; for example, life policies, as at the date of death.

Executors don't have to wait to receive the grant of probate or confirmation to begin this notification and inventory, but a copy must be sent to each institution when it's received from the Probate Registry in England and Wales or the Commissary Department of the Sheriff Court concerned in Scotland. For the initial correspondence, it's sufficient to enclose a copy of the death certificate.

The goal is to get in writing the value of all the assets and debts as at the time of death. This information must be provided on the probate or confirmation forms. Even if an asset is left as a legacy to a beneficiary, it must be listed and accounted for in the inventory. Similarly, you must obtain the value of the deceased's share of any jointly held assets including those passing by survivorship.

Valuing debts

The following is a checklist of debts the deceased might owe. Information on any of these liabilities that apply should be included in page 8 and Schedule IHT419 of HMRC Form IHT 400. This is the return of the testator's whole estate for Inheritance Tax purposes. If necessary, it's generally possible to request a delay in payment of debts until the grant has been obtained and funds are available.

1. Water rates
2. Telecoms bill
3. Pay TV bill

Ask for a bill to the date of death.

4. Electricity bill
5. Gas bill

Take a meter reading on the date of death, or as soon afterwards as possible and ask for a bill to that date.

6. Loan or overdraft

Write to the bank for the outstanding balance.

7. Credit card bills

Write to the credit card company asking for the amount of any outstanding balance.

8. Mail-order catalogue bill

Write to notify the company on the death and to ask whether any outstanding balance is due.

9. Rent arrears
10. Hire purchase payments
11. Debts owed by the deceased to other individuals
12. Outstanding Income Tax and Capital Gains Tax

Reasonable funeral expenses are also counted as a liability of the estate, including the cost of a gravestone; these should be included in page 8 of HMRC Form IHT 400. If the person arranging the funeral is in receipt of Income Support, Working Family Tax Credit or Housing Benefit, he may be able to apply to the Social Fund (a loan-type scheme administered by the Benefits Agency) for a payment to cover reasonable funeral expenses. However, the cost is repaid out of the estate if money subsequently becomes available.

Asset checklist

To help the executors make an inventory of assets, the following checklist itemises some of the typical ones found in an estate. As you go through it, refer to the probate forms which must be filed in England and Wales with the Probate Registry, or in Scotland with the Commissary Department of the Sheriff Court concerned. Not all the assets listed here are specifically categorised on Form IHT 400; those not listed should be recorded on pages 15 and 16 of Form IHT 400 and their total value included in Box 76 on page 7 of Form IHT 400. In Scotland, the application to the Sheriff Court for confirmation (Form C1) includes a full inventory of the deceased's assets and their values. This form can be referred to for its terms where appropriate when completing Form IHT 400, thus avoiding the necessity of duplicating the information already contained in Form C1.

House or flat

If the deceased owned his own home jointly with another person, only the deceased's share of the home is treated as part of his estate. It will usually be a half-share unless the owners held the property as beneficial tenants in common or in some other specific proportions and the title deeds specify that they hold it in unequal shares. If two or more joint owners hold a property in England and Wales as beneficial tenants in common, or in Scotland without a survivorship destination, each person can leave his own share of the property to whomsoever he wishes under his Will. However, if they hold the property in England and Wales as beneficial joint tenants or in Scotland where there is a survivorship destination, the share of a person who dies automatically passes to the survivor or survivors.

If the precise value is not relevant for calculating Inheritance Tax due on the estate (e.g. because the property or the deceased's share of it is to go to the deceased's spouse, and if in the case of a Scottish estate, there is no requirement to calculate the value of the spouse's prior rights on intestacy, see page 26), an approximate value will normally be acceptable. The executor should, however, ascertain as accurate an estimate of value as is reasonably practicable. He may estimate the value himself by reference to the prices which similar properties in the area are fetching, or ask an estate agent for an informal valuation.

In some circumstances, it's better to ask an estate agent or surveyor to make a formal valuation, for which a fee may be charged. For instance, if the property is to be transferred to a beneficiary as part of a legacy instead of cash, (or in Scotland as part of a claim for prior rights) then the executor should have a formal valuation to ensure that the distribution among the beneficiaries is fair.

Whichever method is used, in an estate which is likely to be taxable, the value given will be checked by the District Valuer for HMRC who may challenge it if it appears to be too low. If the property is sold soon after the death (although the executors will not be able to complete the sale until they have the grant showing their entitlement to deal with the property), the District Valuer would normally seek to substitute the sale price for the value submitted in the probate or confirmation application. Details of the property should be included in Schedule IHT 405, Houses, land, buildings and interests in land.

If there is a mortgage on the deceased's house or flat, the mortgage lender should be notified. You should give the deceased's name, address and mortgage account number and enclose a copy of the death certificate. You will need to know how much of the mortgage was outstanding at the date of death, and whether there is a life assurance or mortgage protection policy linked to the mortgage. If there is, you should ask whether the cover is sufficient to repay the mortgage and whether there will be any surplus remaining after repayment.

Bank account

The executors must write to the deceased's bank and, if there is also a building society account, to the building society, with a registrar's copy of the death certificate, to inform them of the death and to instruct them to stop all unpaid cheques and standing orders. You should also ask for a list of all deeds, share certificates and other documents held on the deceased's behalf and the balances on the deceased's accounts (including joint accounts) at the date of death, with a separate figure for interest which had been earned on the money to that date, but not credited to the account. This information is needed for Form IHT 400. It's also useful to ask, in the same letter, what interest has been credited to the deceased's account during the tax year in which he died and whether it was paid net of tax or gross. This information will be needed for the tax return to the date of death.

The executors will also need to open a bank account in their own names to enable them to pay in cheques for the proceeds of sales of assets of the estate, and to write cheques to discharge liabilities. The executors' full names and addresses should be given to the bank, which will send a mandate for completion and signature by the executors.

Any cheques which are made payable to the deceased but which were not paid into his account before the death may be able to be paid into his account or the executors' account, but the bank may insist that such cheques be endorsed in favour of the executors. Once a copy of the grant of probate or confirmation has been shown to the bank, the bank can transfer the balance on the deceased's account to the executors' account.

Stocks and shares

If the deceased owned any shares, the certificates may be at the deceased's home or with his bank, solicitor or stockbroker. If they are at the home and it's to be left unoccupied, it's best to remove them for safe keeping. It may be desirable to check with the registrar of each of the companies in which the shares were held to make sure that the holdings evidenced by the certificates are correct. The name and address of the registrar can usually be found on the counterfoil of the share certificate or you can look them up in the Register of Registrars, a publication which can be found in most reference libraries.

Sometimes, shareholdings are in the nominee name of the shareholder's stockbroker and the stockbroker will have the share certificates. If that is the case, there is no need to write to each of the company registrars, but the stockbroker should be notified of the death and sent a copy of the death certificate.

If any share certificates cannot be found, the executors may need to sign a statutory declaration and indemnity before selling them or transferring them to a beneficiary, for which the registrar of the company will charge a fee. It states that the executors have searched for the certificate and believe it to be lost, and the executors indemnify the company against any loss if the certificate comes to light later in the hands of a person who has a better claim to ownership of the shares than the executors do. Some shareholdings may be uncertificated and therefore no certificates are involved.

Once a complete list of shareholdings has been compiled, the executors can ask a stockbroker for a probate or confirmation valuation, for which he will charge a fee, generally a fixed sum per holding. Alternatively, executors may make their own valuation by referring to the Stock Exchange Daily Official List (SEDOL) for the day the deceased died. The List is available at public libraries or can be bought from the Publications Section of the Stock Exchange in London – see www.londonstockexchange.com.

For probate or confirmation purposes, the value of a stock is the lower of the two values quoted, plus a quarter of the difference between those values; for example, for a share quoted at 96–98p for that day, 96.5p would be the probate or confirmation value.

If any of the shares are quoted 'XD', there is a dividend due to the deceased that has not yet been paid. If you are obtaining a valuation from a broker, he will include such dividends in the valuation. Otherwise, telephone the registrar of the company who will be able to give the value of the dividend. The dividend per share may be a gross figure; in which case multiply it by the number of shares held by the deceased and deduct tax at ten per cent to arrive at the net figure which will appear on the dividend cheque.

The value of unit trust units can be obtained from the fund manager of the relevant unit trust company. If the deceased owned shares in any unquoted companies, write to the company secretary of each one asking for a valuation of the shares at the date of death.

A list of all shares and their values should be included on Schedules IHT 411 and IHT 412. Dividends (the net figure) should be listed separately as shown. Any dividends which were uncashed at the time of death should also be included. The total values are then included in Boxes 62 – 67 on page 7 of Form IHT 400. If the deceased had a personal equity plan (PEP) or an Individual Savings Account (ISA), its provider can give a valuation as at the date of death.

Businesses

If the deceased had an interest in a business, it will need to be valued by the business' accountant, backed up by a copy of the latest three years' accounts and a copy of any partnership agreement, as requested in Schedule IHT 413 of Form IHT 400.

Car

A local garage can provide an accurate valuation of the deceased's car. On the other hand, the executors may prefer simply to sell the car at arm's length on the open market soon after the death and use the sale price as the value at the date of death.

Jewellery

An overall valuation will usually be acceptable for jewellery, although if an individual piece is worth more than £500 it should be valued separately. Similarly, a formal valuation would be prudent in Scotland if the estate is intestate and there are prior and legal rights to be calculated (see page 26). A jeweller can give a valuation, for which he will usually charge a fee. You should tell the jeweller that the valuation is needed for probate or confirmation purposes to ensure you receive an estimate of the price for which he could sell the item, not the replacement value, which may be much higher.

Works of art

One way of finding out whether a particular painting or sculpture is of value is to see if it's separately listed on the deceased's home contents insurance policy, but that is by no means necessarily foolproof. An art dealer can give a valuation of any works of art. Make it clear that you are asking for the price it would fetch at auction at the date of death, not the value for which it should be insured.

Other possessions

There is no need to compile a detailed list of all of the deceased's possessions, including furniture and personal effects. However, if the estate is Scottish and intestate, an auctioneer's formal inventory and valuation of personal effects and household contents will assist the calculation of beneficiaries' entitlements and would be wise. Otherwise, the executor's reasonable and fair estimate of their total value can be given, based on what they might fetch if sold second-hand or, if appropriate, at auction at the date of death, although separate details (and preferably formal valuations) of individual items worth over £500 should be given, as should the values of items such as vehicles, boats and aircraft, antiques, works of art or collections This information should be included in Schedule 407 of the Form IHT 400. HMRC can challenge asset values if they appear particularly low. In the case of a husband and wife, household possessions are generally treated as being held jointly between them, and so their total value should be divided by two to give the value of the deceased's share. Of course, if the deceased owned something outright, the entire value of the item is considered part of the deceased's estate for Inheritance Tax purposes.

National Savings

There is a special procedure for National Savings accounts. The executor must complete Form NSA 904 and send it to the address given on the form for that type of account. For National Savings certificates, the executor will need to write to National Savings asking for a letter confirming the value of the certificates held by the deceased at the date of death. In England and Wales, the Probate Registry will need to see this letter.

Premium Bonds

You must notify the Premium Bonds Office of the holder's death. A form for completion is available at www.nsandi.com, or contact National Savings & Investments on 0500 007 007.

Bonds can either be encashed or they can remain in the prize draw for 12 months after the death. If any prize is won, it can be claimed in the usual way by returning when appropriate the winning bond to the Bonds and Stock Office, and the prize will belong to the estate to be distributed under the deceased's Will, or the intestacy if there is no Will. As long as the value of the bonds and any prize money doesn't exceed £5,000, there is normally no need to provide a copy of the grant of probate or confirmation to receive payment. Premium Bonds are valued at their face value. They should also be listed on the National Savings Form NSA 904.

Outstanding salary or pension payments

If the deceased was employed at the time of death, a letter must be sent to his employer notifying them of the death and asking whether any salary or other payments are outstanding. However, the employer may need to see a copy of the grant of probate or confirmation before paying such payments to the executors.

If the deceased belonged to a union or trade association, there may be a death benefit payable to his family. Likewise, if the deceased was receiving a pension, the scheme administrator or pension provider must be notified of the death and outstanding pension payments claimed.

Outstanding salary or pension payments should be included in Form IHT 400 as an asset of the estate. If the deceased was a member of an occupational pension scheme, a lump sum death benefit may be payable and you should write to the scheme administrator or pension provider to find out if that is the case.

Some benefits payable by an employer or a pension fund may be discretionary and not form part of the deceased's estate on death. This means that they don't pass under the deceased's Will or the intestacy and may not be subject to Inheritance Tax. However, HMRC will require full details of all pension payments and lump sum benefits and these should be provided in Schedule IHT 409 of Form IHT 400.

Life insurance and pension policies

Write to the life insurance company or pension provider to notify them of the date of death, stating the policy number and enclosing a copy of a registrar's copy of the death certificate. Ask what sum is payable on the death and whether it was written in trust for any named person. If it was, the proceeds may be paid direct to that person on production of the death certificate. If not, the proceeds, including any bonuses, will generally be included as part of the deceased's estate and must be included in Schedule IHT 410 of Form IHT 400. Sometimes, the policy will be linked to a loan or mortgage, in which case the proceeds will be paid directly to the creditor, any excess being paid to the estate.

Taxes and bills

If the deceased paid Income Tax under PAYE (Pay As You Earn system) and/or received interest net of tax on bank or building society accounts, there may be a tax refund to claim. On the other hand, if income has been paid gross, or the deceased was a higher rate taxpayer, there may be additional Income Tax to pay. There may also be Capital Gains Tax to pay if, for example, the deceased sold any shares, ,.In any event, the deceased's tax inspector must be informed of the death. He will send a tax return to be completed by the executors, relating to the period up to the time of death.

A refund of Council Tax may be due. The deceased's home will be exempt from Council Tax if it's left empty from the date of death until probate or confirmation has been granted, and for a further six months from the date of the grant. If the death leaves just one other person living in the property, the 25 per cent discount for single occupation may be claimed from the date of death. Any refund of Council Tax in respect of a period before the date of death must be included in Form IHT 400 as an asset of the estate.

Social Security payments

If the deceased was receiving a state retirement pension, the local Department for Work and Pensions office should be notified of the death. The pension book should be sent with your letter inquiring whether there are any pension payments uncollected by the deceased. Any underpaid pension will be a debt due to the deceased and must be included in Form IHT 400 as an asset of the estate. If the deceased was receiving any other state benefits, these will also need to be stopped and any outstanding payments due up to the date of death claimed.

Foreign property

The value in sterling of property owned by the deceased outside the UK or debts owed to him by any resident outside the UK must be reported to the Probate Registry or HMRC in Schedule 417 of Form IHT 400. Inheritance tax can be payable on foreign property if the deceased is domiciled in the UK at the time of death.

Applying for a grant

Excepted/exempt estates

To assist with the proper completion of the applications for a grant of probate or confirmation and the appropriate returns to HMRC (to calculate whether Inheritance Tax is due on an estate), it is first necessary for the executors to determine if the estate qualifies as an 'exempt' estate, or as an 'exempt and excepted' estate, or if neither category applies. This will dictate how to complete certain parts of the applications for a grant and which form is to be used to return the relevant IHT information to HMRC. For Inheritance Tax, the value of the of the estate for probate or confirmation is only one component of the gross estate and if the deceased made substantial gifts during his lifetime, or received income from a substantial trust, or where certain other circumstances apply, this can result in a tax liability even if the IHT tax threshold is not exceeded.

Where the deceased was domiciled in the UK at death, the estate is an 'excepted' estate or an 'exempt and excepted' estate where either:

1. **Excepted estate** – the gross estate for Inheritance Tax does not exceed the excepted estates limit (currently £325,000 and linked to the level of the IHT threshold)

OR

2. **Exempt and excepted estate** – (a) the gross value of the estate is less than £1,000,000 and (b) because all or part of the estate passes to the deceased's spouse who must also be domiciled in the UK, or to a charity

or to other body qualifying as exempt from IHT, after deducting liabilities and those exemptions only, the estate is less than the excepted estates limit

In addition, for both categories all of the following conditions apply:

1. If there are any 'specified transfers' (see below), their total chargeable value does not exceed £150,000.
2. If the deceased had made a gift of land or buildings, it was made to an individual and not to trustees of a trust or to a company and it did not exceed £150,000 in chargeable value.
3. If the estate for Inheritance Tax includes assets held in a trust that are treated as part of the deceased's estate, there is only one such trust and the total value of those assets does not exceed £150,000 (unless the estate is an exempt excepted estate when the value limit is waived).
4. If the estate includes any foreign assets, the total gross value of these does not exceed £100,000.
5. The deceased did not give away any property whilst retaining the benefit of it.
6. The deceased elected that the Income Tax charge should not apply to: (a) assets he previously owned in which he retained a benefit or (b) the deceased's contribution to the purchase price of the assets acquired by another person but in which the deceased retained a benefit.
7. The deceased did not benefit from an alternatively secured pension fund
8. The deceased did not benefit under a registered pension scheme where (a) the benefit was unsecured and (b) they became entitled to the benefit as a relevant dependant of a person who died aged 75 or over.

To qualify as 'specified transfers', the assets given away can only be:

- Cash
- Quoted stocks and shares
- Household and personal goods
- Land and buildings

Any gift of land and buildings only qualifies as a specified transfer if it was an outright gift between individuals. If the gift of land and buildings was to a trust or a company, or the deceased kept back any kind of benefit from the property or was entitled to use it, it cannot qualify as a specified transfer.

If you are not sure whether any transfers made by the deceased fall within these exceptions, you should contact the HMRC Helpline or seek professional legal advice.

Having determined if the estate qualifies as exempt or exempt and excepted, the executors are now in a position to complete the forms appropriately.

The forms – England and Wales

The forms necessary to apply for a grant of probate are available free of charge from the Personal Applications Department of the Principal Probate Registry in London or from the District Probate Registries, see www.hmcourts-service.gov.uk and from HM Revenue & Customs, www.hmrc.gov.uk ; tel: 0845 300 0627.

Depending on the estate of the deceased, the forms to be completed are as below.

1. Form PA1 asks for basic information about the deceased and for the names and addresses of the executors.
2. Form IHT 400 or Form IHT 205 enable the Probate Registry to determine the probate fee and the HMRC any Inheritance Tax and interest.
3. Supplementary pages to be completed with IHT 400 to give HMRC further details of the deceased's assets.

The Probate Registries issue Forms PA1 and IHT 205, whilst HMRC issues Form IHT 400 and its supplementary Schedules. (You will also receive Forms PA2, IHT400 Notes and IHT 206; these contain guidance on completing PA1, IHT 400 and IHT 205, respectively.)

Note: Probate forms must be sent by post to a Controlling Probate Registry; they should not be sent to a local office, even if you want to be interviewed at a local office.

Before looking at the forms in detail, familiarise yourself with the steps and forms involved in obtaining a grant of probate by going through the flowcharts on page 18.

Form PA1 Probate Application Form

Section A asks whether there is a Will and whether a gift is made under it to a person under 18. If so, the executors (or the trustees if the Will appoints trustees) will hold the minor beneficiary's gift until the beneficiary is 18. Question 5 asks for the names of any executors and, if any of the named executors are not applying for probate, why that is the case. If a named executor gives reason D ('does not wish to apply now but may later'), the Probate Registry will provide a power reserved letter for him to sign. Where only one executor is taking out the grant it may be prudent for a non-acting executor to sign a power reserved letter, even if it's not anticipated that he will want to apply at any stage, in case the acting executor dies or becomes incapacitated before the administration of the estate is complete.

Section B asks for details of the deceased's relatives. This will be relevant if there is no Will, as the list of relatives follows the order of entitlement to take out a grant of letters of administration on an intestacy. The list also helps in determining who should inherit where there is an intestacy or a partial intestacy (i.e. where the Will fails to dispose of all the deceased's estate).

Section C asks for details of those applying to take out the grant. The executor whose name and address are given at questions 1-4 will be the first applicant to whom all correspondence will be addressed. There is space underneath for the name and address of the other executors. Questions 7 and 8 ask about the first applicant's relationship to the deceased. This information is needed for the oath which will be sworn at the Probate Registry on application for the grant. More importantly, in the case of an intestacy, this information verifies that the applicant is the person entitled to take out the grant of letters of administration.

Form IHT 205 Short Form of Return of estate information

This form is for use where:

- the deceased died on or after 1 September 2006;
- and the gross value of the estate for IHT is less than the excepted estates limit, or is less than £1,000,000 and there is no IHT to pay having regard to the spouse or charity exemptions only

If you can answer 'no' to all the Preliminary Questions on pages 1 & 2 of this form, there is no need to complete Form IHT 400; continue to answer the questions on pages 3 and 4. If any of the answers to the preliminary questions is 'yes', IHT 400 must be completed, in which case you should answer only the questions on page 2 of Form IHT 205 and send it to the Probate Registry with Form IHT 400. Form IHT 206 contains notes to help you with Form IHT 205.

Form IHT 400 Inheritance Tax Account

See page 19 regarding forms common to England & Wales and Scotland.

The forms – Scotland

Form C1 Confirmation

In every estate where confirmation is needed to uplift or otherwise deal with the deceased's assets, the relevant application form known as Form C1 must be completed by the executor. This form is available online from www.hmrc.gov.uk or free of charge from the Sheriff Clerk's Office of the Sheriff Court in the area where the deceased was domiciled at the date of death – see www.scotcourts.gov.uk.

Form C1 requires the details of the deceased and the executor(s), the declaration of the executor as to the accuracy of the information contained in the form, an Inventory of each item of estate and its value, a summary of the debts/expenses, details of surviving relatives and a summary of the taxable value of the estate with reference where appropriate to the figures contained in the IHT Form 400 relative to the estate. If the estate is taxable, the Form C1 must be stamped by HM Revenue & Customs to show that all tax assessed has been paid, before the Sheriff Court will accept the form and progress the application for confirmation. Guidance Notes (Form C3) are available from HMRC to assist with completion of Form C1. The estate is not taxable if it qualifies as either an excepted estate, or an exempt and excepted estate, but whether taxable or not, a further form must be completed and submitted to HMRC to allow it to satisfy itself as to the position (see below re Form C5 or Form IHT 400).

Form C5 (SE) Information about Small Estates

If the gross value of the deceased's own assets, including his share of jointly held property (but not property passing under a survivorship destination), and including assets that have been nominated to another person during the deceased's lifetime but which are part of the estate (e.g. friendly society funds or a death benefit) is less than £30,000, the estate is called a 'Small Estate' and the Sheriff Clerk will help you to complete the Form C1. The executor is not excluded from the benefits of this procedure even if the value of the estate for Inheritance Tax purposes exceeds the small estates limit as a result of lifetime gifts, gifts with reservation etc. However, even with a small estate, in these circumstances it will still be necessary for the executor to submit the necessary form to HMRC to allow the tax liability to be agreed and Form C5 (SE) is used for this purpose.

Form C5 Short Form of Return of estate information

This form (the Scottish equivalent to the Form IHT 205 for England & Wales) is for use where:

- the deceased died on or after 1 September 2006
- and the gross value of the estate for IHT is less than the excepted estates limit, or is less than £1,000,000 and there is no IHT to pay having regard to the spouse or charity exemptions only

If you can answer 'no' to all the Preliminary Questions on pages 1 & 2 of this form, there is no need to complete Form IHT 400; continue to answer the questions on the remainder of page 2 and on pages 4. If any of the answers to the preliminary questions is 'yes', IHT 400 must be completed, in which case you should stop completing the Form C5 and complete the Form IHT 400 instead.

Guidance Notes C3 cover not only the completion of the Form C1, but also the completion of the Form C5. If only a Form C5 is required, this can be submitted to the Sheriff Court at the same time as the executor submits the C1 and there is no need for the executor to contact HMRC direct. The Sheriff Court takes responsibility for showing the Form C5 to HMRC, whereas it is the executors who must submit a Form IHT 400 to HMRC.

Before probate appointment

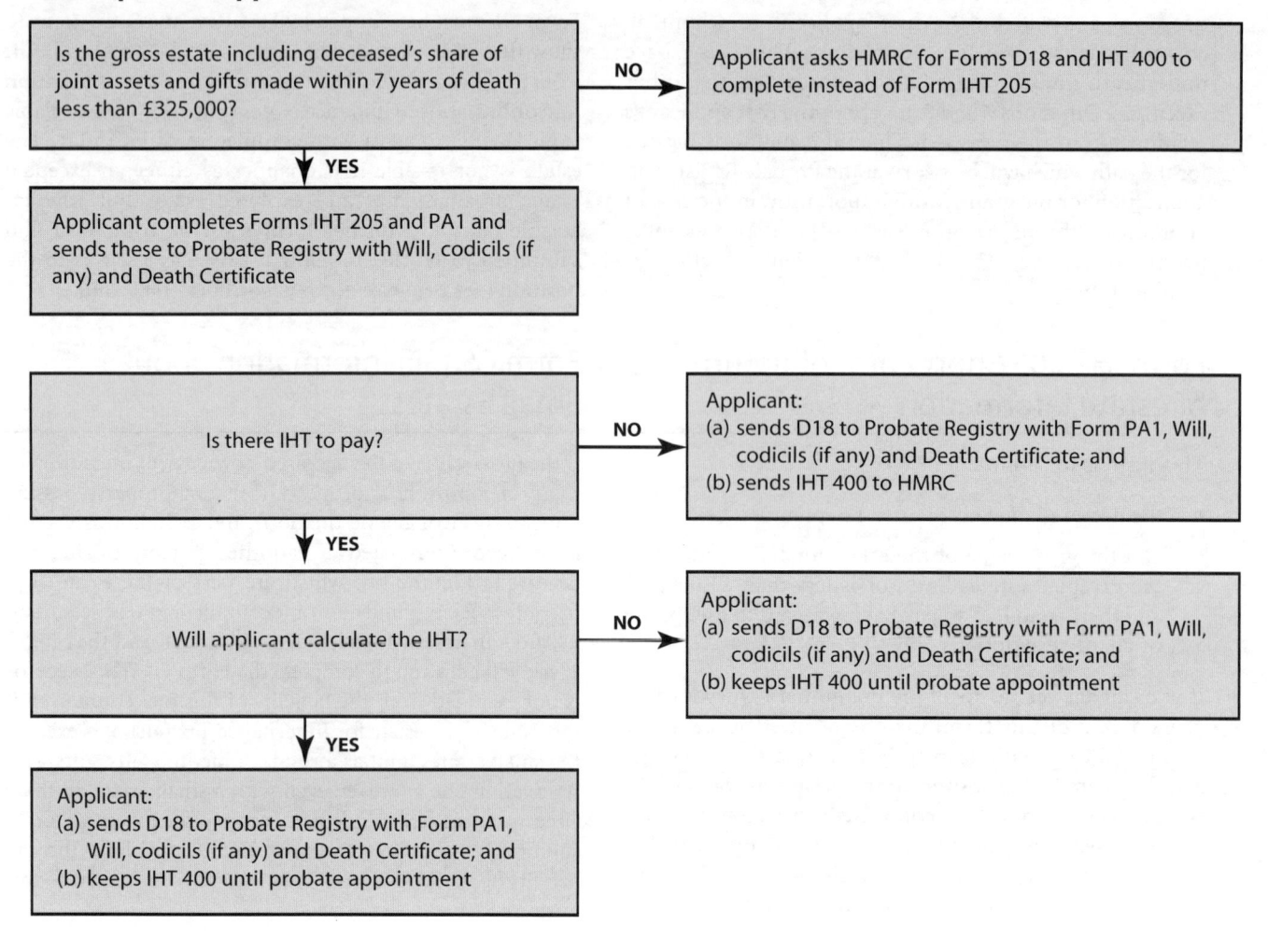

```
┌─────────────────────────────────────┐
│ Is the gross estate including       │         ┌──────────────────────────────────────┐
│ deceased's share of joint assets    │   NO    │ Applicant asks HMRC for Forms D18    │
│ and gifts made within 7 years of    │────────▶│ and IHT 400 to complete instead of   │
│ death less than £325,000?           │         │ Form IHT 205                         │
└─────────────────────────────────────┘         └──────────────────────────────────────┘
               │ YES
               ▼
┌─────────────────────────────────────┐
│ Applicant completes Forms IHT 205   │
│ and PA1 and sends these to Probate  │
│ Registry with Will, codicils (if    │
│ any) and Death Certificate          │
└─────────────────────────────────────┘
```

```
┌─────────────────────────────────────┐         ┌──────────────────────────────────────┐
│                                     │         │ Applicant:                           │
│        Is there IHT to pay?         │   NO    │ (a) sends D18 to Probate Registry    │
│                                     │────────▶│     with Form PA1, Will, codicils    │
│                                     │         │     (if any) and Death Certificate;  │
│                                     │         │     and                              │
│                                     │         │ (b) sends IHT 400 to HMRC            │
└─────────────────────────────────────┘         └──────────────────────────────────────┘
               │ YES
               ▼
┌─────────────────────────────────────┐         ┌──────────────────────────────────────┐
│                                     │         │ Applicant:                           │
│    Will applicant calculate the     │   NO    │ (a) sends D18 to Probate Registry    │
│              IHT?                   │────────▶│     with Form PA1, Will, codicils    │
│                                     │         │     (if any) and Death Certificate;  │
│                                     │         │     and                              │
│                                     │         │ (b) keeps IHT 400 until probate      │
│                                     │         │     appointment                      │
└─────────────────────────────────────┘         └──────────────────────────────────────┘
               │ YES
               ▼
┌─────────────────────────────────────┐
│ Applicant:                          │
│ (a) sends D18 to Probate Registry   │
│     with Form PA1, Will, codicils   │
│     (if any) and Death Certificate; │
│     and                             │
│ (b) keeps IHT 400 until probate     │
│     appointment                     │
└─────────────────────────────────────┘
```

After probate appointment

The probate fee is paid at the probate appointment. If the applicant has completed a Form IHT 205, the Probate Registry will issue the grant by post after the appointment and without any further formalities. However, where the application requires a Form IHT 400, there are further formalities as set out below before the Probate Registry can issue the grant.

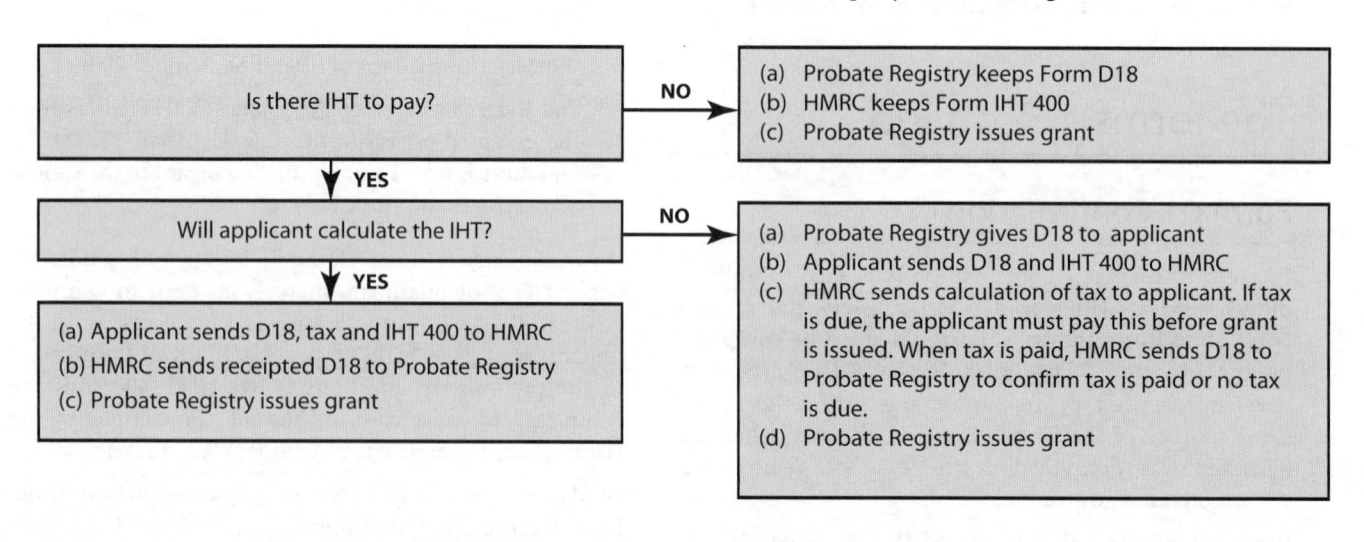

```
┌─────────────────────────────────────┐         ┌──────────────────────────────────────┐
│                                     │   NO    │ (a) Probate Registry keeps Form D18  │
│        Is there IHT to pay?         │────────▶│ (b) HMRC keeps Form IHT 400          │
│                                     │         │ (c) Probate Registry issues grant    │
└─────────────────────────────────────┘         └──────────────────────────────────────┘
               │ YES
               ▼
┌─────────────────────────────────────┐         ┌──────────────────────────────────────┐
│                                     │         │ (a) Probate Registry gives D18 to    │
│    Will applicant calculate the     │   NO    │     applicant                        │
│              IHT?                   │────────▶│ (b) Applicant sends D18 and IHT 400  │
│                                     │         │     to HMRC                          │
│                                     │         │ (c) HMRC sends calculation of tax to │
│                                     │         │     applicant. If tax is due, the    │
│                                     │         │     applicant must pay this before   │
│                                     │         │     grant is issued. When tax is     │
│                                     │         │     paid, HMRC sends D18 to Probate  │
│                                     │         │     Registry to confirm tax is paid  │
│                                     │         │     or no tax is due.                │
│                                     │         │ (d) Probate Registry issues grant    │
└─────────────────────────────────────┘         └──────────────────────────────────────┘
               │ YES
               ▼
┌─────────────────────────────────────┐
│ (a) Applicant sends D18, tax and    │
│     IHT 400 to HMRC                 │
│ (b) HMRC sends receipted D18 to     │
│     Probate Registry                │
│ (c) Probate Registry issues grant   │
└─────────────────────────────────────┘
```

Form IHT 400

If the facts of the case dictate that a Form IHT 400 must be completed, (i.e. Form C5 in Scotland or Form IHT 205 in England are not appropriate) guidance notes are again available from HMRC's website to assist. This Form comprising 16 pages and separate Schedules numbered IHT 401 – IHT 421 enables you (and HMRC) to determine whether any Inheritance Tax is payable. Not every Schedule will require completion depending on the deceased's circumstances. There is more information about this Form in the section below referring to forms common to both Scotland and England and Wales.

If Inheritance Tax is payable on a Scottish estate, then payment should be submitted to the HMRC Accounts office at HM Revenue & Customs, Accounts Office, St Mungo's Road, Cumbernauld, Glasgow, G70 5WY. If there is tax to pay, you will need an IHT reference number and a payslip before you make the payment. Fill in Form IHT 422 and send it to the address shown on that form or apply online.

The Forms IHT 400 and Form C1 should both be submitted in the first instance to HM Revenue & Customs, Inheritance Tax, Ferrer's House, PO box 38, Castle Meadow Road, Nottingham, NG2 1BB. The Form C1 will be receipted by the HMRC and returned to you, allowing you to apply for confirmation from the Sheriff Court

If you are using the IHT Direct Payment Scheme (DPS) in terms of which the deceased's bank released funds direct to HMRC to meet the tax, complete Form IHT 423 and send this to the deceased's bank at the same time.

Bond of caution

In the case of an application for confirmation by an executor-dative in an intestate estate, before applying it's normally necessary for a bond of caution to be obtained from an insurance company. This bond of caution is effectively a guarantee given by the insurance company to the court that the executor-dative will distribute the deceased's estate properly in terms of the law of intestate succession. For such a bond of caution a single premium is payable which is likely to be in the region of £300 or more depending on the values and circumstances. In granting such a bond of caution, the insurance company may require certain conditions to be complied with (such as the need to obtain clearance from the Department of Work and Pensions that there has been no overpayment of benefits or that a minor beneficiary's share of the estate should be held until the beneficiary attains the age of 16).

Where the executor-dative is the spouse of the deceased, and if the spouse's prior rights exhaust the whole of the intestate estate of the deceased (see ??), then only the spouse is entitled to seek appointment as executor-dative and there is no requirement for a bond of caution.

Application for confirmation – Scotland

Application for confirmation is made to The Sheriff Clerk of the Sheriff Court in the area in which the deceased had been domiciled at his death by:

1. Form C1 (receipted where Inheritance Tax is payable).
2. Form C5 (where no tax due and estate is excepted or exempt & excepted.
3. Will (docquetted with reference to the Form C1) or bond of caution, as appropriate.
4. Letters of declinature from any surviving executor named in the Will and not wishing to accept office (docquetted with reference to the Form C1).
5. The appropriate fee, currently:

    for a gross estate under £5,000: nil.

    for a gross estate not exceeding £50,000: £200.

    for a gross estate exceeding £50,000: £200.

    A charge of £5 is payable for each certificate of confirmation requested.
6. Request for confirmation and any required certificates of confirmation.

The forms – England, Wales & Scotland

Form IHT 400 Full Inheritance Tax Return

Applies to estates both in England and Wales and in Scotland.

The questions on this form are similar to those on the English Form IHT 205 and the Scottish Form C5, but they require fuller details. This form must be completed if the estate is not exempt or exempt and excepted. There may be a number of supplementary pages to complete with the Form IHT 400. If there is insufficient space for all the information asked for, you should attach a separate sheet of paper and include the total on Form IHT 400 itself. The Guidance Notes available from the HMRC website will help you complete the form. If the estate includes land or buildings in the deceased's sole name, Schedule IHT 405 should also be completed. If it includes stocks and shares, list the details on Schedule IHT 411 and IHT 412. Schedules IHT 403, IHT 418 and IHT 409 deal with gifts, assets held in trust and death benefits payable under pension policies respectively. These may not appear to be part of the estate, but they may need to be taken into account in order to calculate Inheritance Tax. Schedule IHT 404 deals with jointly-held property including land and buildings. Overseas land and buildings and other foreign property should be included in Schedule IHT 417.

The Inheritance Tax on some types of property may be paid by instalments. Page 11 of the form includes a box to be ticked, should you wish to do that.

The executors have the choice of either calculating any Inheritance Tax themselves or leaving it to HMRC to work out and the appropriate box should be ticked on page 11 of the form.

All the executors should read the Declaration on page 12 of Form IHT 400 and sign it. (NB this differs from the Form C1 and the Form C5 in Scotland which need to be signed by one executor only.)

Schedules Form IHT 411 & Form IHT 412 Stocks and Shares

If the deceased owned stocks or shares, the details of those holdings should be entered in the appropriate Schedules depending upon whether the assets are UK government securities, listed stocks and shares (not giving control of the company), unlisted stocks and shares and control holdings.; only the totals from each Schedule are carried to Boxes 62 – 67 on page 7 of Form IHT 400.

The Schedules tell you the order in which you should list the holdings and where to show dividends.

Schedule IHT 405 Houses, land, buildings and interests in land

Complete this form if the deceased owned a house or any land or rights over land such as fishing rights in his sole name; only the total amount will be carried to Boxes 68 and 70 on Form IHT 400. The notes at the top tell you what to put in each column. If the property is let, attach copies of the tenancy agreements.

The Schedule for the 'Open Market Value'; don't deduct the amount of any mortgage which has been or will need to be repaid. If the deceased owned, for example, the house in his sole name, record the gross value of the entire property, even if the spouse or someone else is claiming an interest in part of it. The debt of the mortgage will be recorded elsewhere on the form.

If the deceased was a joint owner of the property, you should complete Schedule IHT 404 and include the value of the deceased's share where requested.

This is not an exhaustive discussion of all parts of the Form IHT 400 and its Schedules and we have covered only some of the most commonly applicable sections. In the event that you encounter difficulty in completion of the Form, the HMRC guidance notes are very helpful, or you may wish to seek the advice of a solicitor experienced in this field.

At the Probate Registry – England & Wales

About three weeks after sending the probate forms, as set out in the flowcharts, the executors will be contacted with a time and date for an interview. All executors need to attend in order to swear an oath, which is needed to apply for the grant of probate. They will also need to produce the testator's original Will. Where the executors have completed a Form IHT 205, this is signed at the probate registry interview.

Probate fees must be paid at this interview. It may therefore be necessary for executors to arrange for a loan or overdraft to pay these fees and the Inheritance Tax due on the issue of the grant. Probate fees may be paid by cheque, banker's draft, postal order or in cash. On personal applications, the probate fee is currently £130, unless the net estate is less than £5,000, in which case no probate fee is payable for the grant.

At the interview, the executors will be asked to swear that the information on the oath and HMRC account is correct. It's a good idea to take back-up files to verify facts and figures. If all the information is exactly as the executors have previously submitted, they are asked to sign the account, swear to the facts set out in the oath, which refers to the Will and put their signatures on the Will. Then the commissioner handling the case adds his signature to the oath and Will. The executors may then order as many copies of the grant of probate, each bearing the court's seal, as are necessary to notify all the parties first informed of the death with copies of the death certificate. Copies currently cost £1 each. If there are further questions before the grant can be issued, the executors could be asked to return to the registry for another interview.

In the case of intestacy, the grant issued is a 'grant of letters of administration'. The administrator should order as many copies of the grant as are necessary, as above.

If there is no Inheritance Tax due, the grant will be issued almost immediately. Assuming there are no further questions, the grant of probate with a copy of the Will attached and the copies of the grant will arrive by post. The grant is proof to the public that the executors can realise the deceased's assets, collect from the deceased's debtors and distribute the assets as determined by the Will. Both the Will and the grant of probate are public documents.

The executors can now send a grant of probate to all parties that first received the death certificate, requesting whatever money is due to be sent to the executors. This money is deposited into the executors' bank account, from which debts of the deceased are paid.

At the Sheriff Court – Scotland

Within about two weeks after submitting your application for confirmation to the Sheriff Clerk in the Sheriff Court concerned, the Sheriff Clerk will send to you the confirmation (together with any certificates of confirmation ordered).

The grant of confirmation is proof to the public that the executors can realise the deceased's estate, collect from the deceased's debtors and distribute the assets, as determined by the Will. Both the Will and the grant of confirmation are public documents. The executors can now send the confirmation, or a certificate of confirmation, to all parties concerned, requesting whatever money is due to the estate. This money can be deposited into the executors' bank account from which debts of the deceased can be paid.

Inheritance tax

The executors can calculate the tax themselves by working through the Form IHT 400 Calculation sheets and completing the Form IHT 400 accordingly. If the executors are not sure how to complete Form IHT 400, the Inheritance Tax Helpline (tel: 0845 30 20 900) can be contacted for assistance in completing the form or visit the HMRC website at www.hmrc.gov.uk/inheritancetax.

If the executors don't wish to calculate the tax, HMRC will do this for them (see flowcharts on page 18 for details).

HMRC exempts all property left to the surviving spouse or to charity, and the first £325,000 (the tax threshold or 'nil rate band') of the estate not left to the spouse or charity (assuming there have been no gifts made by the deceased in the seven-year period prior to death; if there have been any gifts in the seven-year period before death, you should declare these in Schedule IHT 403 to Form IHT 400). The executors should note that the available tax threshold may be increased if it is appropriate, to apply the new rules relating to utilising the unused Inheritance Tax threshold of a predeceasing spouse (the 'transferable nil rate band'). The excess bears tax at 40 per cent. If the total value of all lifetime gifts in any one tax year doesn't exceed £3,000, then they will all be free of Inheritance Tax. If the total value of gifts in any tax year is less than £3,000, then the surplus of this relief can be carried forward to the next tax year only and be used against gifts made in that later tax year, once the £3,000 available for the later tax year has been used up. This relief is known as the annual exemption.

Inheritance Tax owed on buildings or land, a business or a share in a business, shares giving a controlling interest in a quoted company and some unquoted shares can, with prior approval, be paid in ten equal annual instalments (although interest is payable on these instalments if the asset is land or buildings). Inheritance tax on other assets must be paid before the grant of probate or confirmation can be issued and interest is charged on any Inheritance Tax outstanding from the end of the sixth month after the death (except where it's being paid by non-interest bearing instalments).

Changes to the amount of Inheritance Tax

Even after probate or confirmation has been granted, HMRC may ask further questions about the assets and liabilities of the estate, and values may have to be negotiated. For example, HMRC may challenge the value reported on Form IHT 400 for a house or for unquoted shares. This could result in more Inheritance Tax being payable.

If the executors discover an asset or debt of the deceased which they didn't know about before they applied for probate or confirmation, they must report it to HMRC as soon as possible after its discovery. This may also change the amount of Inheritance Tax payable.

Once the Inheritance Tax position has been settled, the executors should ask HMRC for Form IHT 30, an application for a 'clearance certificate' confirming the executors to be discharged from further Inheritance Tax. Two copies completed and signed by all the executors are needed by HM Revenue & Customs. One copy is returned certifying that no further Inheritance Tax is payable. The executors can then distribute the estate. However, if any further assets come to light subsequently, these too will need to be reported to HM Revenue & Customs, as the discharge from Inheritance Tax would not cover them nor the situation where a further tax liability arises from a deed varying the disposition of the estate

Raising money to pay Inheritance Tax and the probate fee or confirmation dues

Because an executor cannot draw on the funds in the deceased's bank account until he can show entitlement by producing the grant, the executor may need to borrow the necessary funds to pay Inheritance Tax and the probate fee or confirmation dues. There are, however, some assets which an institution may be willing to release before the grant of probate or confirmation is available, in order to pay the Inheritance Tax, and some assets that may be realised without producing the grant of probate or confirmation. The tax may be covered, or partly covered, from such sources as an alternative to borrowing. The following are assets which the executors may be able to use in this way.

1. **National Savings.** In England and Wales, and in Scotland, if the deceased had a National Savings account, National Savings certificates or Premium Bonds, National Savings may issue a cheque in favour of HMRC to cover the Inheritance Tax payable on the estate or part of it. The executors should explain to the probate registry at their interview that they would like to use funds of the deceased's National Savings account to pay the tax. The registry will issue a note stating that the executors have made a personal application and showing the amount of probate fees and Inheritance Tax payable.

   The registry then sends this note to the relevant National Savings office, which will send the cheque for the tax and the probate fee to the probate registry directly. Any remaining balance on the deceased's National Savings account will be paid to the executors and any remaining National Savings certificates and Premium Bonds can be encashed once the grant has been obtained.

2. **Funds payable to others without grant of probate or confirmation** (see 'Is a grant of probate

or confirmation necessary?' on page 10). Consider utilising funds from nominated property, joint property or lump-sum death benefits from pension funds, life assurance companies and friendly societies which have been written in trust for another person. However, such funds or assets would belong to the person to whom they are payable, rather than to the estate, and the executors would need to borrow from that person if they wished to use those funds to pay the Inheritance Tax.

3. **Pension funds and friendly societies.** Funds of up to £5,000 from some pension funds and friendly societies.

4. **Banks and building societies.** Banks and Building societies are often willing to release money to pay Inheritance Tax and the probate fee or confirmation dues, and may have agreed to be part of HMRC's Direct Payment Scheme ('DPS'). The executors should complete the DPS form IHT 423 and submit one such form to every bank from which funds are required. (You must firstly obtain an IHT reference number from HMRC to include on the form. When HMRC receive the funds from the bank(s) they will link this with the IHT 400 submitted by the executors and will stamp and return the Probate summary (or in Scotland, the Form C1).

5. **Other assets.** Furniture and other personal possessions of the deceased may be sold by executors, who are entitled to sell the assets of the estate from the date of death, but in England and Wales, not administrators, who are only entitled to do so once they have the grant of letters of administration.

6. **Stocks and shares.** If held through a stockbroker's nominee company, subject to the stockbroker's agreement

If insufficient assets are realisable before the grant is issued, the executors will have to borrow the money to pay the Inheritance Tax. Some sources might include:

1. **Loan from the deceased's bank.** A bank will normally make a loan to the executors, although a fee will be payable based on the size of the loan and, of course, interest will be charged. The executors may claim Income Tax relief on the interest payment for the first year of the administration in respect of a loan for the Inheritance Tax payable on personal property.

2. **Loan from a beneficiary.** A beneficiary may be able and willing to lend the money to the estate to pay the Inheritance Tax, particularly if the bank interest and fee would be paid out of cash that he would otherwise receive.

Administering an estate

Distribution of gifts and legacies

To satisfy any debts of the estate, it's the assets forming part of the residuary estate that are used first. If there are still outstanding debts when the residuary estate has been used up, cash legacies are reduced proportionately to meet the debt. If there are unpaid debts outstanding, specific items left as legacies under the Will need to be sold. Once all the debts are paid and the assets are all accounted for and collected the executors are in a position to distribute the estate in accordance with the Will.

As each personal effect, gift and legacy of money is distributed to the beneficiaries of the estate, the executors should ask each beneficiary to sign a receipt. The receipt should record the amount of money or description of the gift, the names of the executors, the name and signature of the beneficiary and the date. The beneficiary should be invited to keep a copy of the receipt. The Will may contain a clause saying that, if there is a gift to a child, his parent or guardian can sign the receipt. Otherwise, gifts to minors should be invested by the executor in an account until the child reaches 18 or 16 in Scotland (the age of 'majority') or the age of inheritance specified in the Will, which could be higher.

Transfer of assets

If assets are to be transferred to a beneficiary (rather than being sold and the proceeds paid to him), the method of transfer will differ according to the asset. Household and personal effects may be physically handed over, without any legal paperwork.

Shares will need to be transferred using a Stock Transfer Form (available to purchase and download from www.lawpack.co.uk or by request from the relevant company registrar's office). This should be completed and signed by all executors and sent to the registrar of the company, together with the share certificate and an office copy of the grant of probate, or certificate of confirmation, as appropriate. Alternatively, a stockbroker or bank would be able to prepare the stock transfer forms and send them to the registrars. If a shareholding is to be split between two or more beneficiaries, a separate form of stock transfer is needed for each beneficiary. No stamp duty is payable on the transfer of shares from executors to a beneficiary, provided that the appropriate certificate on the back of the form has been completed and signed by the executors. If the shares are registered in the name of a stockbroker's or bank's nominee company, the executors need not complete stock transfer forms but should write to the nominee company, giving it the name and address of the beneficiary of the shares and instructing it to hold the shares on behalf of the beneficiary in future.

If a house or flat is to be transferred to a beneficiary, the procedure in England and Wales differs according to whether the title is registered or unregistered.

In the case of registered land title(s) in England and Wales, you need to use Land Registry Form AS1 Assent of Whole of Registered Title(s). If only part of the registered land title is being transferred, you will need to complete a Form AS3. Forms are available from www.landreg.gov.uk. The completed form needs to be signed by each executor in the presence of a witness and by the beneficiary to whom the property is being transferred. The executors should then send it, together with an office copy of the grant of probate, the land certificate and the Land Registry fee to the Land Registry so they can register the new owner. The Land Registry fee will vary according to the value of the property, net of any outstanding mortgage (if it has not been repaid following the death). The current scale of fees for registering an assent is as follows:

Value net of mortgage	Fee
£0–£100,000	£40
£100,001–£200,000	£50
£200,001–£500,000	£70
£500,001–£1,000,000	£100
£1,000,001 and over	£200

If the land is in England and Wales and unregistered, the title deeds will consist of a number of deeds and documents including the deed (a conveyance) whereby the property was transferred to the deceased. In the case of unregistered land it's best to seek the advice of a solicitor as the title to the property would then have to be registered at the Land Registry as a first registration application.

In Scotland, whether the title of heritable property (i.e. land or buildings) in Scotland is registered in the Land Register (of Scotland) or not, a docket on the confirmation or certificate of confirmation can be a method of transferring title to a beneficiary (either under a Will or in terms of legal rights or in accordance with the law of intestate succession in Scotland). The confirmation or certificate of confirmation with completed docket should be held with the titles of the property. It may be prudent for preservation purposes to have such docketed confirmation (or certificate of confirmation) registered in the Books of Council and Session on application to:

The Keeper of the Registers of Scotland
Meadowbank House
153 London Road
Edinburgh EH8 7AU.

A docket isn't needed if the title deed contains a survivorship destination, as the title will automatically have transferred to the survivor on the death of the first to die.

It should be noted that a docket will suffice as a 'link in title' to allow the beneficiary to sell the asset at a later date, or bequeath it under his own Will, but as the beneficiary's title has not been registered in the Land Register of Scotland, there may be problems at a later date if for example the beneficiary wishes to use the property as security for a loan. If the beneficiary wishes to ensure that the entitlement is a matter of public record and that all the usual benefits of full ownership apply, the beneficiary may prefer that the executors execute a formal disposition in his favour instead of a docket. This will incur registration dues (based on the property value) when the disposition is registered in the Land Register, but this would normally be treated as an expense of the estate.

Final accounts

The careful records that have been kept since the date of death should now be organised in a neat and easily-read format for approval by each beneficiary.

A word of caution: In England and Wales, for a period of six months following the grant of probate, claims may be made under the Inheritance (Provision for Family and Dependants) Act 1975; for example, by a member of the deceased's family who feels he has not been properly provided for in the Will. In England and Wales, it's therefore wise not to distribute the residue of the estate until six months have passed. If such a claim is made, the executors should seek the advice of a solicitor.

In Scotland, it may also be prudent to delay distribution of the estate until the expiry of six months after the death to allow for any claims to be made against the estate. If the executor were to distribute prior to the expiry of that six-month period, he may be personally liable for any claims intimated in that period. Additionally, where a deceased died intestate while cohabiting unmarried, or in a relationship with the same characteristics except that the parties were of the same sex, it is open to the cohabitee to make a claim against the estate within six months of the date of death. If such a claim is foreseeable, the executors should not consider distributing the estate to other beneficiaries within that period.

After the residuary beneficiaries (or those entitled under the intestacy laws) have signed off on the accounts, the estate is completed. The executors' bank account can be closed and whatever money remains is given to those entitled under the Will or intestacy laws.

Paperwork should be kept on file for 12 years after final distribution. In the event that the deceased left someone a life interest or liferent in the estate, or the Will created any other form of ongoing trust, the paperwork should be kept for 12 years after the final distribution to whoever inherits after the death of the last person with a life interest or liferent.

In Scotland, the principal papers such as the deceased's Will, confirmation, final accounts and beneficiaries' receipts should ideally be retained indefinitely, particularly where there is a continuing trust.

Taxation of the estate

Income from the estate will be liable to Income Tax from the date of death to the date it has been fully administered. The estate will be assessed to Income Tax on all income received gross at the basic rate, but with no personal allowance. No further Income Tax will be payable if all income (e.g. bank interest, dividends, etc.) has been paid net of tax. Gains (relative to date of death values) on any sales of shares after death may be liable to Capital Gains Tax. The executors' annual exemption for Capital Gains Tax is the same, for the tax year in which the death occurred and the following two years, as any individual's annual exemption (currently £10,100). However, gains in an estate are taxed at 28 per cent. Thus the executors should liaise with the beneficiaries before selling assets which are likely to make a taxable gain to see whether the Capital Gains Tax can be reduced by using the beneficiaries' rates of tax and exemptions. If in doubt, the executors should seek professional advice.

When the executors notify the Tax Inspector for the deceased's tax district of the death, the Inspector may send Form R27 Potential Repayment to Estate which asks for information as to whom will be entitled to the residue of the estate, whether there will be any trust continuing after the estate has been wound up and whether the executors expect to receive any untaxed income or make any capital gains. On the basis of that form, the Inspector will either issue a tax repayment, or request that a full self-assessment return is made for the deceased for the tax year to date of death in order to assess any tax due.

The executors may also need to issue a certificate of tax deduction (Form R185 (Estate Income), also available from the tax office) to the beneficiary who is entitled to the residue of the estate. This form shows the gross income received by the estate during the tax year, the tax paid by the executors on that income and the resulting net figure. As long as the residue isn't held in trust, the income of the estate is treated as the income of the beneficiary, who will report the income on his tax return, and Form R185 (Estate Income) is evidence that tax has already been paid on it. If the beneficiary is a non-taxpayer, he can reclaim the tax. If he is a higher rate taxpayer, he will be assessable to additional tax.

Succession on intestacy

If a person dies without making a Will, or if their Will is invalid, they are intestate. The management of their estate, which is their house (if any) and other assets minus their debts and liabilities, is then placed in the hands of administrators (called executors-dative in Scotland) appointed by the court, who are likely to be close members of the deceased's family.

In England and Wales, the administrators distribute the deceased's estate according to the rules of intestacy established by the Administration of Estates Act 1925; these apply to anyone whose domicile or permanent home at the time of death is England or Wales, or in some cases to one whose home is abroad but who retains English domicile.

In Scotland, the rules of intestacy, established by the Succession (Scotland) Act 1964 as amended, apply to anyone whose domicile or permanent home at the time of death is Scotland or in some cases to one whose home is abroad but who retains Scottish domicile.

In effect, these rules allow the deceased's surviving spouse and dependants to claim their property and money without regard to any verbal expression of wishes the deceased may have made. Only by making a Will can a testator ensure that his wishes will be given effect to on death. If no surviving relatives can be found, the deceased's entire estate goes to the Crown.

The rules of intestacy in England and Wales

The rules of intestacy are complex. The effect of the rules depends partly on the size of the deceased's estate. If their estate is large, less may go to their spouse. Broadly speaking, funeral expenses and administration costs are deducted from their estate. The remaining property is distributed as follows:

1. If only the deceased's spouse survives them, he receives all of the property remaining in the estate, provided that he survives for 28 days after their spouse's death.

2. If the spouse survives the deceased by 28 days and the deceased is also survived by children

    a. the surviving spouse receives:

    i) a 'statutory legacy' of up to £250,000 plus the interest accrued from the time of death until payment. The statutory legacy is free from tax and costs.

    ii) all household and personal items of the deceased ('personal chattels').

    iii) a trust (called a 'life estate') consisting of half of the estate after the initial £250,000 and the personal chattels have been deducted. The spouse is said to have a 'life interest'; that is, he is entitled to receive income for life from this trust, but may not spend the capital.

    b. the children receive:

    i) half of the remaining estate divided equally among them.

    ii) the right to inherit, upon the death of the surviving spouse, the half of the estate in which that spouse had a life estate. This life estate is divided equally among the surviving children. If any of the children have predeceased the deceased, leaving their own child/children, their child/children will automatically take their parent's share by substitution.

3. If the spouse survives the deceased by 28 days and, instead of children, there are parents, brothers, sisters, nieces and/or nephews

    a. the surviving spouse receives:

    i) up to £450,000 plus the interest accrued from the time of death until payment.

Succession on intestacy in England and Wales

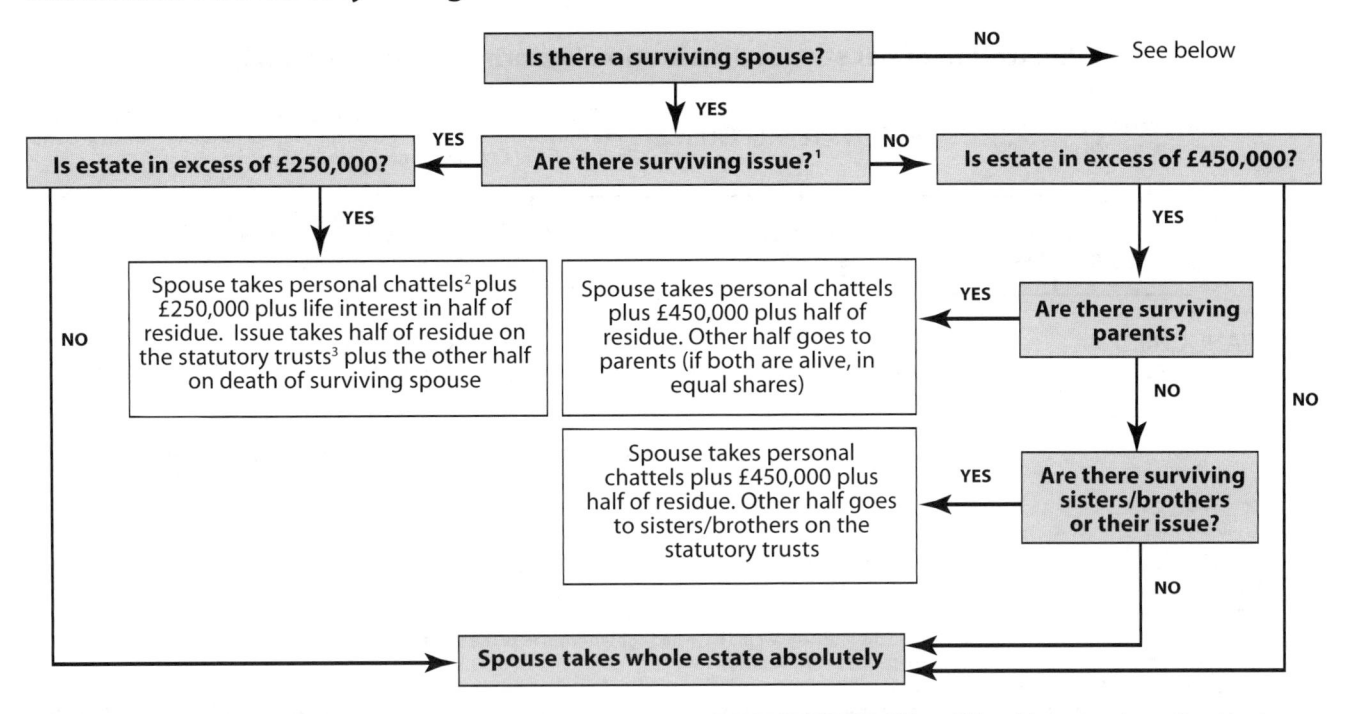

Is there a surviving spouse? → NO → See below
↓ YES

Are there surviving issue?[1]
- YES → **Is estate in excess of £250,000?**
  - YES → Spouse takes personal chattels[2] plus £250,000 plus life interest in half of residue. Issue takes half of residue on the statutory trusts[3] plus the other half on death of surviving spouse
  - NO → Spouse takes whole estate absolutely
- NO → **Is estate in excess of £450,000?**
  - YES → **Are there surviving parents?**
    - YES → Spouse takes personal chattels plus £450,000 plus half of residue. Other half goes to parents (if both are alive, in equal shares)
    - NO → **Are there surviving sisters/brothers or their issue?**
      - YES → Spouse takes personal chattels plus £450,000 plus half of residue. Other half goes to sisters/brothers on the statutory trusts
      - NO → Spouse takes whole estate absolutely
  - NO → Spouse takes whole estate absolutely

---

1 'ISSUE' Children, grandchildren or remoter lineal descendants of the intestate.

2 'PERSONAL CHATTELS' Under s.55 (1) (x) of the Administration of Estates Act 1925, 'personal chattels' includes: horses, motor cars, garden implements, domestic animals, furniture, linen, china, glass, books, pictures, musical and scientific instruments, jewellery, household and personal articles, food and drink, but does not include any chattels used at the date of death for business purposes nor money or securities.

3 'THE STATUTORY TRUSTS' Those children of the intestate who are alive at his or her death inherit in equal shares although if a child is under 18 he or she must reach the age of 18 or marry under that age in order to inherit. If any child dies before the intestate, leaving children of his or her own, those children (i.e. the intestate's grandchildren) will take per stirpes i.e. they will take their parents' share equally between them (provided they reach the age of 18 or marry under that age). If remoter issue predeceased the intestate leaving their own issue, this process would continue down the generations. References to the children of the intestate should be read as references to brothers, sisters, aunts or uncles as appropriate, where any of those classes are stated to inherit on the statutory trusts. See illustration of per stirpes distribution on page 26.

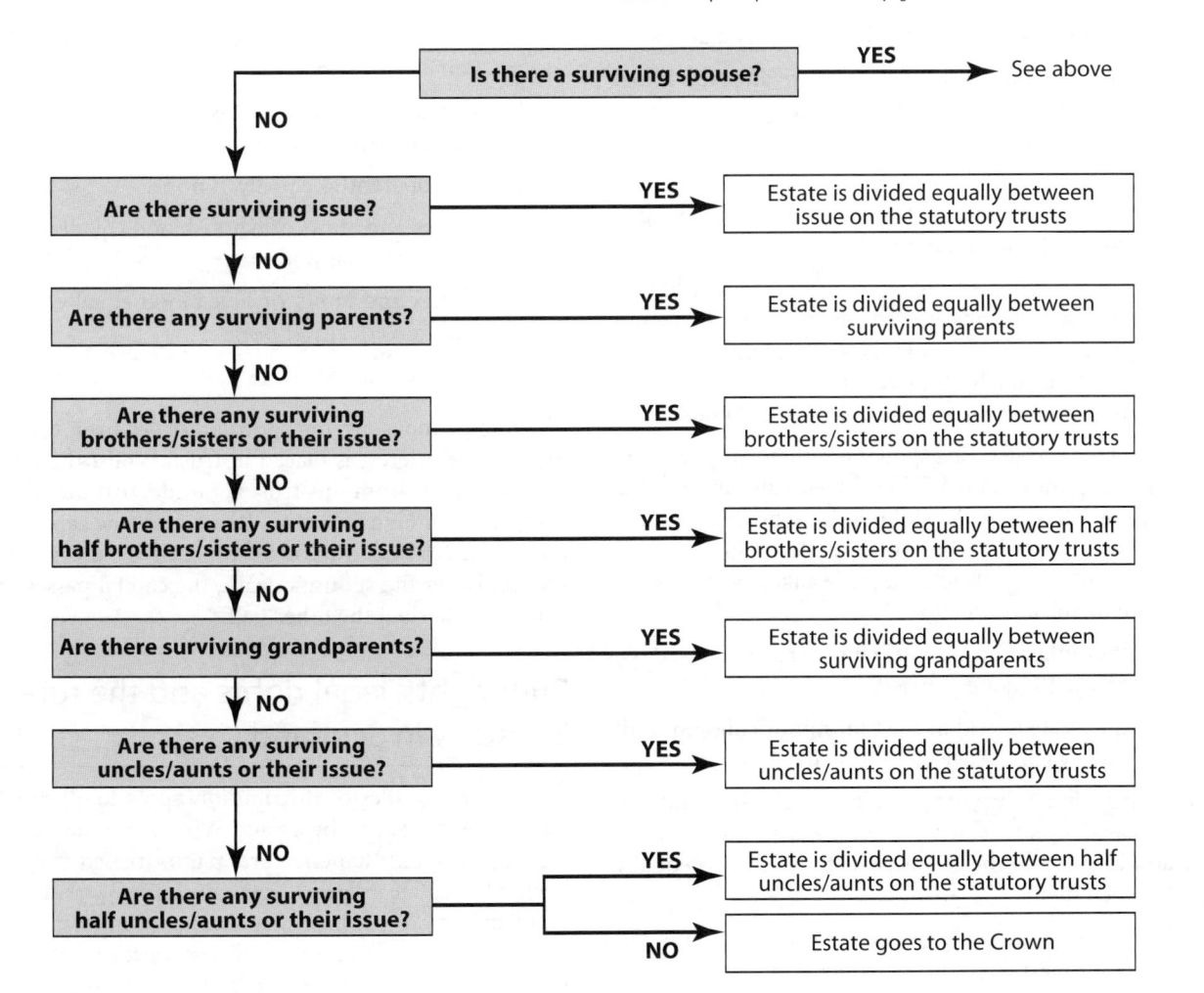

Is there a surviving spouse? → YES → See above
↓ NO

Are there surviving issue? → YES → Estate is divided equally between issue on the statutory trusts
↓ NO

Are there any surviving parents? → YES → Estate is divided equally between surviving parents
↓ NO

Are there any surviving brothers/sisters or their issue? → YES → Estate is divided equally between brothers/sisters on the statutory trusts
↓ NO

Are there any surviving half brothers/sisters or their issue? → YES → Estate is divided equally between half brothers/sisters on the statutory trusts
↓ NO

Are there surviving grandparents? → YES → Estate is divided equally between surviving grandparents
↓ NO

Are there any surviving uncles/aunts or their issue? → YES → Estate is divided equally between uncles/aunts on the statutory trusts
↓ NO

Are there any surviving half uncles/aunts or their issue?
- YES → Estate is divided equally between half uncles/aunts on the statutory trusts
- NO → Estate goes to the Crown

Succession on intestacy in England and Wales (continued)

Illustration of per stirpes distribution (ignoring inheritance tax)

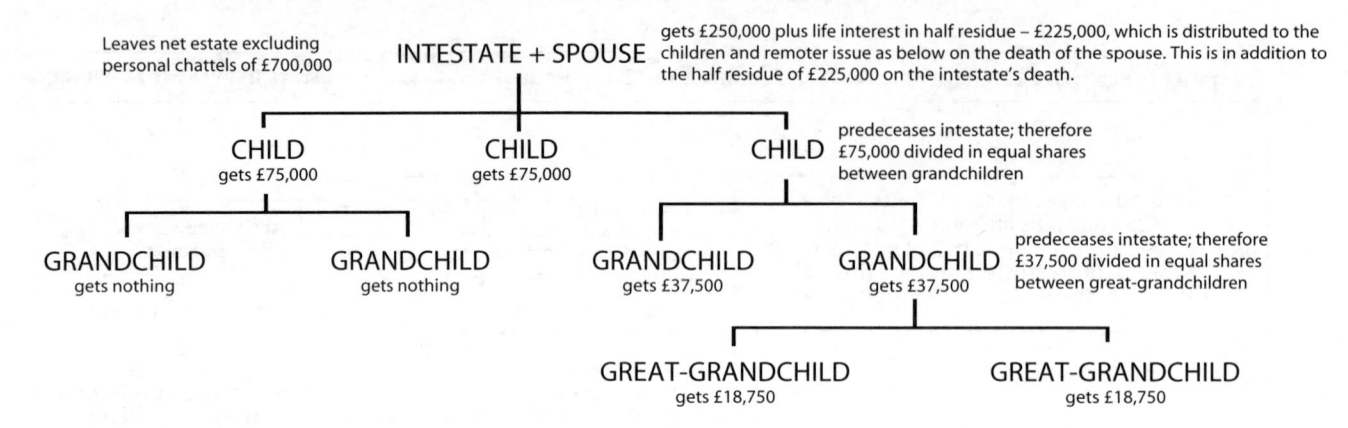

Leaves net estate excluding personal chattels of £700,000

INTESTATE + SPOUSE gets £250,000 plus life interest in half residue – £225,000, which is distributed to the children and remoter issue as below on the death of the spouse. This is in addition to the half residue of £225,000 on the intestate's death.

- CHILD gets £75,000
- CHILD gets £75,000
- CHILD predeceases intestate; therefore £75,000 divided in equal shares between grandchildren
  - GRANDCHILD gets nothing
  - GRANDCHILD gets nothing
  - GRANDCHILD gets £37,500
  - GRANDCHILD gets £37,500 — predeceases intestate; therefore £37,500 divided in equal shares between great-grandchildren
    - GREAT-GRANDCHILD gets £18,750
    - GREAT-GRANDCHILD gets £18,750

NOTES

1. **Representation**
   Where any person who, if he/she had survived the intestate, would have had right to any part of the intestate estate has predeceased the intestate but has left issue who survive, such issue shall have their parent's right to the estate.
2. **Succession of collaterals (brothers and sisters)**
   Where brothers and sisters of an intestate, or of an ancestor of an Intestate have right to any part of the intestate estate, collaterals of the full blood shall be entitled to succeed in preference to collaterals of the half blood. Where collaterals of the half blood succeed, they rank without distinction as between those related to the intestate through their father or their mother.
3. **Succession in cases of illegitimacy**
   No distinction is drawn between succession by legitimate or illegitimate issue of the intestate.

---

ii) all household and personal items of the deceased.

iii) absolute title to half of the estate after the initial £450,000 and the personal chattels have been deducted.

b. the deceased's surviving parents receive absolute title to the other half of the estate, to be divided equally between them.

c. f there are no surviving parents, the other half of the estate is inherited absolutely by brothers and sisters of the whole blood equally, or their children equally. If there is none, the entire estate, however large, goes to the deceased's spouse.

4. If there is no surviving spouse but there are surviving children, the estate is divided equally among the children. If any of the children have predeceased the deceased, leaving their own child/children, their child/children will automatically take their parent's share by substitution.

   a. they inherit immediately if they have achieved the age of 18 or are married.

   b. the estate is held in trust for minor children until they reach the age of 18 or marry.

5. If there is no surviving spouse or children but the deceased is survived by their parents, they receive absolute title to the entire estate to be divided equally between them.

6. If there is no surviving spouse, children or parents, the estate is inherited in the following order:

   a. brothers and sisters equally, or their children equally, if none
   b. half-brothers and half-sisters equally, or their children equally, if none
   c. grandparent(s) equally, if none
   d. uncles and aunts of whole blood equally, or their children equally, if none
   e. uncles and aunts of half blood equally, or their children equally, if none
   f. the Crown.

The money the surviving spouse receives from the estate under a life interest is placed in trust. Whilst the right to receive interest from this trust is for life, that interest isn't likely to be enough to live on. Remember, the capital must remain intact and cannot be touched by the surviving spouse. Upon the spouse's death, the capital passes on to whoever inherited the other half.

Prior rights, legal rights and the rules of intestacy in Scotland

The following rules of distribution apply to all property that is not dealt with by a valid Will. It should be noted that certain entitlements are paid/satisfied from the heritable estate (land and buildings) and other entitlements are paid/satisfied from net moveable assets (e.g. cash, shares, insurance policies, motor vehicles, etc). In order to calculate the rights of the relevant parties, the executors must correctly identify which assets are heritable and which are moveable, before accounting to the intestate beneficiaries appropriately.

The executors must separately calculate values and assets due to the three categories of beneficiary who may benefit under intestate succession (1) prior rights claimant, (2) legal rights claimants and (3) claimants entitled to the 'free estate'.

1. All debts and funeral expenses and all and any liability for Inheritance Tax are paid out of the deceased's estate.

2. If the deceased's spouse survives, then he or she will be entitled to 'prior rights' comprising:
   a. a dwellinghouse (subject to any burdens affecting it) in which the spouse was ordinarily resident at the date of the deceased's death up to the value of £300,000 (or cash of £300,000 if the dwellinghouse has a greater value than £300,000, to be satisfied entirely from the heritable estate);
   b. furniture and plenishings (moveable goods) up to the value of £24,000;
   c. a cash sum: if the deceased leaves issue, the amount of £42,000 and if they leave no issue, the amount of £75,000. These sums are to be satisfied proportionately from the value of the moveable and heritable estate remaining after satisfaction of prior rights a. and b. Interest is payable on the cash sum from the date of death to date of payment at a rate of 7 per cent.

   If the intestate estate is not sufficient to meet the prior rights, the surviving spouse may be entitled to the whole intestate estate. A divorced spouse or former civil partner has no entitlement to prior rights.

   After satisfaction of prior rights, the executors must then attend to a separate category of rights known as legal rights which relate only to the deceased's net moveable assets (everything apart from land and buildings). It should be noted that legal rights apply both to intestate and testate cases. The deceased may make a Will which excludes his spouse and/or children, but they may if they wish claim their entitlement to legal rights and it is the executors' duty to inform any potential claimant of their rights. However, in testate cases where the legal rights claimant has been left a legacy under the Will, the claimant must chose between legal rights and the legacy and may not have both. You will see that it is virtually impossible for a testator to ensure that no benefit can pass to a spouse or children.

3. If the spouse and issue survive, the legal rights fund is divided in the following manner:
   a. one-third to the deceased's spouse; and
   b. one-third to the deceased's issue (their children and the issue of predeceasing children).

   The remaining one third is included in the 'free estate' referred to below.

4. If the deceased leaves no spouse, but does leave issue, then half of the legal rights fund is due to the deceased's issue.

   The remaining half is included in the 'free estate' referred to below.

5. If the deceased leaves no issue, but does leave a spouse, then half of the legal rights fund is due to the deceased's spouse.

   The remaining half is included in the 'free estate' referred to below.

   After satisfaction of prior rights and legal rights, what is left in the estate (being the balance of any heritable property not due in satisfaction of prior rights and the balance of moveable property not due in satisfaction of prior rights and legal rights) is historically referred to as the 'free estate' or 'dead's part'. Effectively, this is the part of the deceased's estate he would have been free to dispose of by Will, or which otherwise passes under the rules of intestate succession. The order of succession to the free estate is as follows, with the entitlement passing to the next in line, only if there is no one surviving in the earlier categories to inherit:
   a. If children or remoter issue survive the deceased, they take the whole intestate estate.
   b. If either or both, the deceased's parents and brothers and sisters, the surviving parent or parent takes one half of the free estate and the surviving brothers and sisters the other half.
   c. If brothers and sisters survive but not parents, they take the whole free estate.
   d. If parents but not brothers and sisters survive, the parents take the whole free estate.
   e. If a spouse survives he/she will take the whole.
   f. If uncles and aunts survive (being brothers and sisters of either parent of the deceased), they take the whole.
   g. If a grandparent or grandparents survive (being a parent or parents of either parent of the deceased), they take the whole.
   h. If brothers and sisters of any grandparent survive, they take the whole.
   i. If there are no survivors under the foregoing categories, ancestors of the deceased remoter than grandparents, generation by generation successively, without distinction between maternal and paternal lines, shall take the whole. Failing ancestors of any generation, the brothers and sisters of those ancestors have right to the whole, before ancestors of the next more remote generation.
   j. If no one survives under the above categories, then the free estate will go to the Crown as the ultimate heir (known in legal terms as the ultimus haeres).

The following principles also apply to the succession to the intestate estate in Scotland:

- Representation applies at every level such that if no primary beneficiary survives, but leaves issue surviving the deceased, such issue will take the parent's share and only if there is no issue, with the share pass to the next category of beneficiary.
- The preference for succession through the male line no longer exists.
- Collaterals (i.e. brothers and sisters) of the full blood will inherit in preference to collaterals of the half blood.

A mistress, common-law wife, spouse separated by a formal separation agreement and a divorced spouse have no right to inherit under the laws of intestacy (except as previously stated in Scotland where a cohabitee may potentially have a claim on an intestate estate). In England and Wales, a spouse separated by an order from the Magistrates' Court does retain the right to benefit under the laws of intestacy.

It's also possible for someone to die partially intestate. This occurs if a person fails to deal with all of their property in their Will, or if a beneficiary dies before the person and they haven't provided for that contingency. If any part of the inheritance cannot be given to another beneficiary named under the Will, that part must be distributed according to the laws of intestacy

Succession on intestacy in Scotland to the 'dead's part' or 'free estate'

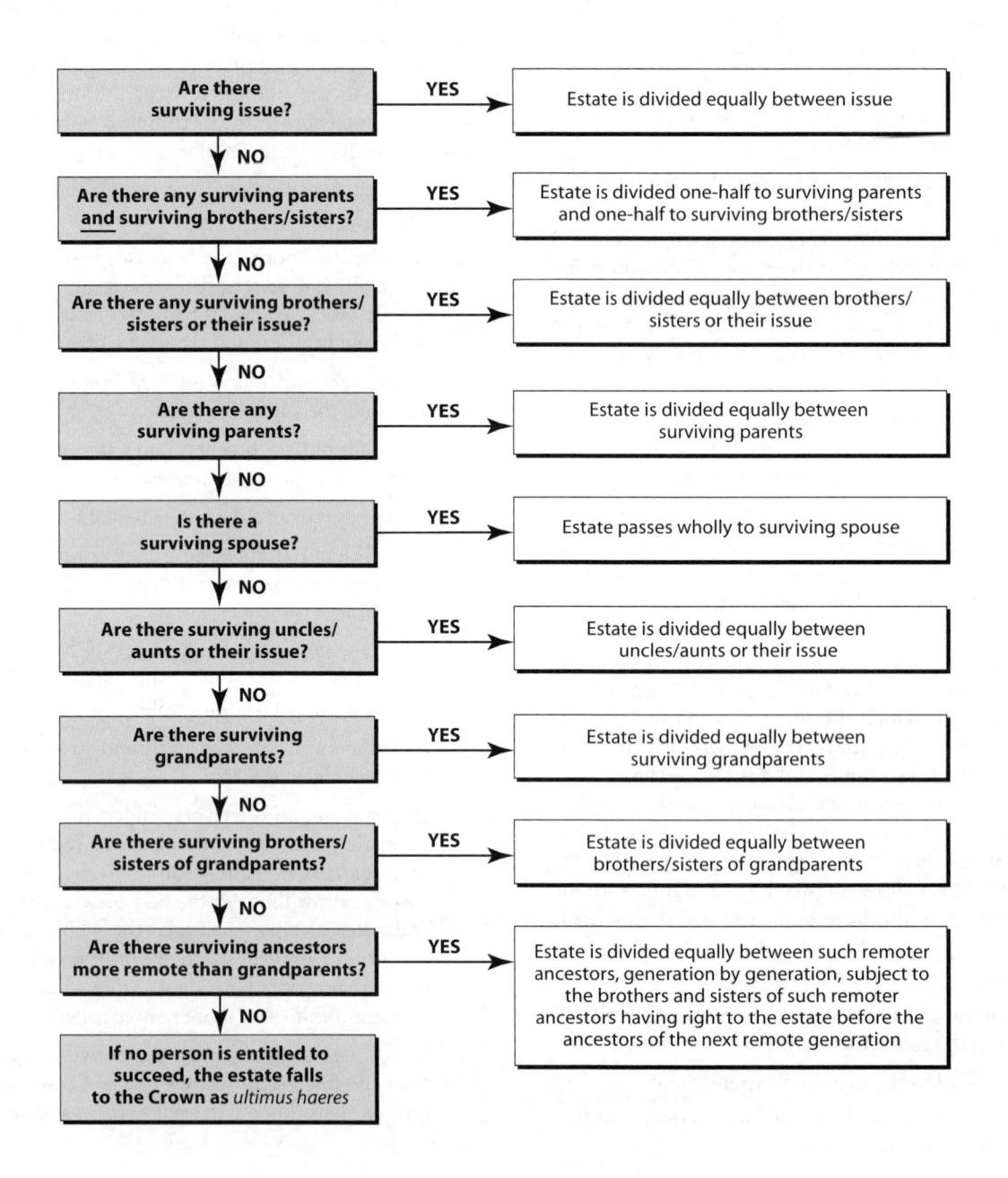

Question	Answer	Outcome
Are there surviving issue?	YES	Estate is divided equally between issue
Are there any surviving parents and surviving brothers/sisters?	YES	Estate is divided one-half to surviving parents and one-half to surviving brothers/sisters
Are there any surviving brothers/sisters or their issue?	YES	Estate is divided equally between brothers/sisters or their issue
Are there any surviving parents?	YES	Estate is divided equally between surviving parents
Is there a surviving spouse?	YES	Estate passes wholly to surviving spouse
Are there surviving uncles/aunts or their issue?	YES	Estate is divided equally between uncles/aunts or their issue
Are there surviving grandparents?	YES	Estate is divided equally between surviving grandparents
Are there surviving brothers/sisters of grandparents?	YES	Estate is divided equally between brothers/sisters of grandparents
Are there surviving ancestors more remote than grandparents?	YES	Estate is divided equally between such remoter ancestors, generation by generation, subject to the brothers and sisters of such remoter ancestors having right to the estate before the ancestors of the next remote generation

If no person is entitled to succeed, the estate falls to the Crown as *ultimus haeres*

An overview of probate/confirmation

1. Register the death and obtain copies of the death certificate.
2. Attend to the funeral, burial, cremation, etc.
3. Find and review the deceased's Last Will & Testament or establish if the deceased died intestate; and in Scotland identify the beneficiaries on intestacy or any beneficiaries with a legal rights entitlement in a testate estate.
4. Determine who the executors are and whether they are able and willing to act. If not, or if the deceased didn't leave a valid Will, determine who will act as administrators of the estate or as executors-dative. Get the agreement of the personal representatives in writing.
5. a. In England and Wales, apply to the Personal Application Department of the most accessible and convenient probate registry for the forms required.
   b. In Scotland, application for confirmation (the Scottish equivalent of probate) is made to the Commissary Department of the Sheriff Court serving the area in which the deceased was domiciled at the time of death, which may be different from the place where the deceased died; for example, the death may have occurred in a hospital away from the area in which the deceased was domiciled. (NB If the deceased was domiciled outside Scotland or if the domicile isn't known, then the application has to be made to the Commissary Office of the Sheriff Court in Edinburgh.) The required application forms for confirmation can be obtained from the Sheriff Clerk concerned or from the HMRC website.
6. Secure the house and/or other property of the deceased, insuring the house, car and any other valuable items as necessary.
7. Organise yourself for valuing assets, corresponding with others, keeping financial records and receiving the deceased's mail. Open an executors' bank account.
8. Write to all financial and business organisations in which the deceased had an interest. Include a copy of the death certificate and request the necessary information for the probate or confirmation application and the returns to HMRC
9. List the deceased's assets and liabilities. Review them. Is it necessary to apply for a grant of probate or confirmation? If the estate appears to be insolvent or there are other complexities, see a solicitor.
10. If the estate appears to be worth more than £325,000, (or where it exceeds the higher value available after application of a predeceasing spouse's available Inheritance Tax allowance) make arrangements to raise money (e.g. by borrowing or selling some of the deceased's personal property) to pay Inheritance Tax before the grant of probate or confirmation can be issued. Consider raising the funds from the deceased's own account using the Inheritance Tax Direct Payment Scheme.
11. Fill out probate or confirmation forms as information is collected and return them to the Probate Registry or Sheriff Court concerned. In Scotland, the form of application for confirmation is a Form C1. Complete a Form C5 (in Scotland) or a Form 205 (in England and Wales) if the estate is either excepted or exempt and excepted. However, if the estate is neither an excepted estate nor an exempt and excepted estate then it's necessary for Form IHT 400 to be completed and submitted to HMRC prior to applying for confirmation.
12. a. In England and Wales, when the Probate Registry contacts the executors, all executors visit the Registry or local office to sign or swear the necessary forms and pay probate fees.
    b. In Scotland, it's not necessary for the executors to attend at the Sheriff Court concerned as one of the executors can complete the necessary Form C1 which is the application for confirmation and mail it to the Sheriff Court concerned. If the deceased didn't leave a Will, then normally it's necessary for a bond of caution (an insurance indemnity) to be obtained from an insurance company and lodged with the application for confirmation, once the separate petition has been made to the court for the appointment of the executor(s) dative. Such a bond of caution would not be required if there was a surviving spouse as the deceased's estate would pass to that spouse in terms of the law of intestate succession in Scotland. (N.B. The premium for any required bond of caution is likely to be of the order of £300 or more depending on values and circumstances.)
13. Pay any Inheritance Tax due at the time of application and arrange for instalment payments if any of the assets qualify.
14. The Probate Registry or Sheriff Court concerned sends the grant of probate or confirmation to you by post along with in England and Wales any additional probate copies (sealed copies) ordered or in Scotland certificates of confirmation. (N.B. In Scotland, a certificate of confirmation relates to one specific item of estate.)
15. Send copies of the grant of probate or the appropriate certificate of confirmation to each organisation contacted in Step 8 to show the executors' entitlement to deal with the deceased's assets. In return, organisations release the deceased's assets to the executors and close or transfer the deceased's accounts and files.
16. Advertise for creditors, if necessary. If any large or unexpected claims result, you should consider consulting a solicitor.

17. Respond to any queries raised by HMRC concerning the values of assets or liabilities of the estate. Agree final figures with them. Report any additional assets or liabilities that have come to light since probate or confirmation was granted.

18. When all assets are collected, pay debts, including any unpaid Income Tax and Capital Gains Tax relating to the deceased's income up to the time of death.

19. Ask the Inspector of Taxes for an Income Tax return or repayment claim form and complete it with details of the income of the estate to the end of the tax year during which the deceased died. Pay any tax due. A return may also be needed for each subsequent tax year if the administration of the estate isn't complete within one tax year.

20. Ask the HMRC for Form IHT 30 (Application for a Clearance Certificate); complete it and have it signed by all the executors and in due course receive the signed discharge certificate from the Revenue.

21. Check that there have been no claims against the estate (in England or Wales under the Inheritance (Provision for Family and Dependants) Act 1975) during the six months following the grant of probate or confirmation and that there were no claims made by cohabitees in a Scottish estate in the six months after date of death In Scotland, settle any claims for legal rights arising in testate cases; if legal rights are to be renounced by the entitled parties, obtain formal discharges, to be placed with the estate papers. Barring any such challenges, the estate can be distributed.

22. When all the assets have been accounted for and debts paid, legacies can be distributed. Get a receipt from each beneficiary.

23. Draw up estate accounts. Get approval of the accounts from all residuary beneficiaries (or those entitled under the intestacy laws) and send them copies. Make payment of final balance of residue due to beneficiaries. Issue HMRC Form R185 (Estate Income) to the residuary beneficiaries showing their shares of the income of the estate and the tax deducted from it during the tax year.

24. When all cheques have cleared, close the executors' account.

25. The administration of the estate is now complete. All accounts should be saved for 12 years, or in Scotland, indefinitely along with the other principal estate papers.

© 2011 Lawpack Publishing Limited
76-89 Alscot Road, London SE1 3AW
www.lawpack.co.uk